W9-BLY-951

Plugged In™

StepLiving
FOR Teens

Getting Along With
Stepparents, Parents,
and Siblings

Written by

oel D. Block, Ph.D and Susan S. Bartell, Psy.D

PSS!
PRICE STERN SLOAN

To my family, Gail my wife, Abbey and Fred, my son and daughter. You have brought me closer to a feeling of being complete.—J.B.

To Lew, my magic, and to Max, Gillian and Mollie, our future teens.—S.B.

Text copyright © 2001 by Joel Block and Susan Bartell. All rights reserved. Published by Price Stern Sloan, a division of Penguin Putnam Books for Young Readers, New York. Printed in the United States of America. Published simultaneously in Canada. No part of this publication may be reproduced, stored in any retrieval system, or transmitted, in any form or by any means, electronic, mechanical, photocopying, recording, or otherwise, without the prior written permission of the publisher.

Library of Congress Cataloging-in-Publication Data is available.

ISBN 0-8431-7568-0 (PB)

0-8431-7569-9 (GB)   A B C D E F G H I J

Plugged In™ is a trademark of Price Stern Sloan, Inc.
PSS! is a registered trademark of Penguin Putnam, Inc.

Contents

- I hate going to my dad's house since he got married because there are tons more rules. What can I do?

49 chapter 3: Stepsiblings and New Babies

- My dad disciplines me much more strictly than my stepmother's kids.

- My stepbrother won't stay out of my stuff, no matter how many times I ask. It's driving me crazy!

- My stepmother obviously favors her own children. Is this unfair?

- I worry that my stepfather and his kids are more important to my mom than I am.

- I'm jealous because my dad's stepkids get to spend more time with him than I do.

- My mother and stepfather are having a baby. Will they forget about me?

79 chapter 4: Always Stuck in the Middle

- My mom criticizes my stepmother, and my dad gets upset if I don't take his side against my stepfather. I'm caught in the middle because I don't want to hurt anyone's feelings.

- I feel guilty having fun with my father and stepmother because my mom always quizzes me about it. It makes me uncomfortable. How do I get her to stop?

- My dad discusses everything I tell him with my stepmother.
  I can't trust him to keep a secret anymore.

96 chapter 5: This Really Isn't Working for Me

- My stepfather acts like I'm in the way, and we argue all the time.
  But my mom doesn't even realize it's happening.

- My stepmother changed everything in my dad's house—
  from wallpaper to towels. It was fine the way it was, and she's
  ruined it.

- My mom and I used to spend lots of time together. Now we
  always have to include my stepdad and his kids. I really miss our
  private time.

- My stepmother tries so hard to be nice that it gets on my
  nerves. How can I tell her without hurting her feelings?

- My dad married his affair and they expect me to be happy for
  them. I hate her, and I'm furious with him. So get real, Dad!

- My dad left the family because there was so much fighting. So
  why can't I leave this stepfamily for the same reason?

119 chapter 6: Sorting Out Confusing Feelings

- Sometimes I wish my father and stepmother would divorce, and
  my parents would get back together. The truth is that everyone
  is happy the way things are now, so why do I feel this way?

- I always compare my real parent to my stepparent. I don't know how to stop myself.

- When my dad and stepmom argue, I am afraid they will also get divorced.

- My mom always closes the door when she and my stepdad are alone in their room. She used to leave it open all the time, so now I feel shut out. Why do they need so much privacy?

- My parents say they will always love me, even though they are remarried, but how can I be sure? After all, they used to love each other, right?

- My stepfather wants to adopt me, and I'm not sure how I feel about it.

150 chapter 7: Money Is a Huge Issue

- My mom complains that my dad doesn't give her enough child support but he seems to spend a lot on his new wife.

- My stepbrother's real father buys him tons of things that I don't have. It's not fair that he lives with us but gets all that stuff from his dad.

- My dad says he can only pay for part of my college tuition because he's also paying for his stepkids' college. They're not his real children, so why do I have to lose out?

- My dad used to buy me whatever I wanted. But his new wife told him he's spoiling me, so now he doesn't even want to pay for a school notebook. Why is she suddenly in charge of his money?

Introduction

"I *finally* got used to living with one parent, and now this . . . a stepfather and a *stepfamily*. I don't have clue number one how this will end up." Kelly, who expressed these feelings, was really confused and frustrated. Sound familiar?

Like Kelly, if you have started reading this book, you're probably in a stepfamily, or about to become part of one. It also means that you've already been through a lot in your life. Your parents may be divorced, or one of your parents may have died. You've likely done more crying, yelling, and fighting than many kids you know. And now, here you are *again*, in the middle of another confusing situation—having to adjust to a stepfamily. Of course, there can be many benefits to having a stepfamily. For example, now you have two parents who can drive you everywhere! But, seriously, adjusting to a new family can be very difficult. It can feel like this for months or even years. Teenagers often find it more difficult to get used to a stepfamily than younger children do because it's tougher for an older kid to make changes in his or her life. One of the hardest things about being a teenager in a stepfamily is that you don't have much control over all the big changes that come with having a stepparent and maybe stepsiblings. It was hard enough getting used to living with only one parent. It can be even more frustrating to be told that the life you have finally become used to is changing again, like it or not!

Whether you've been in a stepfamily a long time or you're just getting used to the idea of your mom or dad living with someone else, there are many questions you probably don't know how to answer. For example, you may be confused about who is supposed to make the rules in the house, or whether you should even have to listen to your stepparent's rules. You may be thinking you don't have enough privacy and wondering how you can change that. There are probably lots of other things that you think about, too. You might not want to discuss these things with your parents or stepparents. In fact, it's even possible that they don't have all the answers.

Here's something that you may want to think about. Even though there are lots of kids who haven't been through all the stuff you're dealing with, there are many, many others (millions, actually) who are in the same position as you. There are other kids whose mothers or fathers have re-married, kids who have stepbrothers or stepsisters, and kids who have new babies in their stepfamilies. Some of them like their stepfamilies, and some don't. These teenagers are just like you, with the same experiences, frustrations, and concerns. Many of them have asked the same questions as you, and some of them have even figured out the answers.

Now, that's where we come in. We are psychologists who work with stepchildren and their families, and one of us was a stepchild (it's Dr. Block, if you're wondering). After doing this kind of work for a long time, we decided the best way to help teenagers understand their stepfamilies was to speak with teenagers who are in stepfamilies. So we asked teens to tell us the concerns and questions they have had in their families. We also asked what they and their families have done to answer the questions or resolve the problems. The next thing we did was to look at all the advice and suggestions we have given over the years to teenagers and their stepfamilies. We figured out which advice has worked well and which hasn't.

You may find that certain things covered in this book don't apply to you, but reading about them might make you think of a friend's situation. So, by reading the book you may be able to offer help to a friend. By the time you finish reading this book you will have a much better understanding of many of the confusing and frustrating things that happen in your stepfamily. You will also realize that you are not alone. You may even find out that living in a stepfamily can be a positive experience, at least most of the time!

Chapter One
First Things First

Your questions begin when you find out your parent is remarrying. It's definitely a confusing time so don't be surprised if you're not sure whether to be happy or sad.

My mom is getting remarried. I'm scared and angry and I don't know why.

Kenny: I can't believe this is happening to me—I'm going to be a *stepchild!* How awful is *that?*

Kenny got along well with his mom's boyfriend, James, and had been excited that she and James would eventually marry—at least until now! Kenny didn't realize that, like most teenagers, his feelings are on a constant roller coaster. One look from a crush can send you flying, and then a C on a quiz can make you furious. Well, what about when something huge happens, like a parent getting married again? Like Kenny, you should expect to have many different feelings about it. After all, this change isn't just happening to your parent, it's happening to you as well.

If you like the person your parent is marrying, you'll probably be excited and happy. But at the same time, you might feel upset or angry for all sorts of reasons. Kenny was upset by the word "stepchild." The label made him feel there was something different and embarrassing about him. He imagined other kids would think his family was weird, and he would have to tell everyone he was a stepchild. But there is no rule that you have to think of yourself as a stepchild. You're still the same person you always were; you just have another parent. And besides, if you like your stepparent, now you'll be related to someone whom you want in your life.

Of course if you don't like your stepparent,

things will be much more complicated. It's not unusual to have negative feelings about a stepparent because they're taking the place of your real parent in some way. But if this is the only reason you don't like your step, perhaps you're not giving him or her a fair chance.

For example, Vicki met her dad's girlfriend six months after her parents' divorce. They went out for dinner, and Vicki thought Brenda was nice enough. But later talking with her best friend, Vicki described Brenda as ugly, annoying, and uncool. She hated that her dad was dating and wouldn't give Brenda a break. But over time, Vicki realized Brenda was really trying, so she decided to give her a chance. It wasn't easy, but a year later when her dad and Brenda married, Vicki went with Brenda to choose a gown and helped with the wedding plans.

Sometimes when parents begin a new romance, they focus on their own happiness, forgetting how the relationship is affecting you. This is understandable because love can change anyone's perspective. You can't just expect your parent to

know how you feel. It's up to you to let your mom
or dad know. At first, Kenny didn't tell his mom he
was confused because he was afraid it would hurt
her feelings. But Kenny's tense feelings increased, and
one day they had a huge fight about the wedding.
Finally, he explained his conflict about her getting
married. Initially she was upset because she thought
that he was going to cause trouble between her and
James. But Kenny assured her that he liked James
and was just nervous about the changes. Kenny
made his mom see just how confused he really was.

With this new understanding from his mom,
Kenny could begin to see the upside of the
marriage. Sometimes real feelings come out only
during or after a fight. So fights can be good. But it's
possible, and usually better, to share your feelings
without fighting, especially when the other person has
no clue you're even upset.

What if it doesn't work . . . ?

What if you *really* don't like your new stepparent, no
matter how hard you try? You're still going to have

to do your best to get along. You don't want
to alienate yourself from your parent, who obviously
loves you but loves this person, too. Also, you
don't want to start out the wrong way with your
stepparent who will be in your life for a long time.
So your best bet is to keep an open mind. Keep
communicating with your parent and try not to
allow negative feelings to interfere with the
possibility of building a relationship with your
stepparent. Your parent doesn't love you less
because he or she is marrying someone, so don't
feel sorry for yourself. Rather, work on trying to
improve things at home.

I told my mom she shouldn't get married, but she did anyway. Don't you think it's unfair to me?

Haley: It is so obvious that this "new family" is going to be a mega-disaster and my life will be wrecked. Why can't I have a say in decisions that affect me?

We posed Haley's question to a few stepteens and were surprised that not everyone agreed with Haley. Alex thought that all teenagers, not just stepteens, are put in situations where they can't make important decisions. Good point! It's really hard when you're not a kid but you're not an adult yet. This means, like it or not, the adults aren't always going to include you in big decisions. Alex explained, "Haley's gotta realize her mother doesn't *have* to ask her for permission to get married, even if it is going to affect Haley's life." Hmm, an interesting point. Can you honestly say you would ask permission to get married if you were a middle-aged adult? But it would be awesome if Haley could share her feelings with her mother, and of course it would be equally great if her mom understood her feelings. Even if her mom has already decided to get married, Haley should still clear the air. If her mom knows what she's worried about, they may be able to work some things out so the new family is not a mega-disaster.

Carla, another stepteen, saw things differently from Alex. "This marriage is going to have an effect on Haley's life, and if Haley was upset, her mom should have waited until Haley moved out before getting remarried," she argued.

"But what if Haley never moves out?" demanded Alex. "I mean, she may stick around for years figuring out her life, or put off leaving *because* she wants to prevent her mom from getting married!" Actually, Alex is right. Sometimes when teenagers are angry with a parent for wanting to remarry, they deliberately do things to make their parent's relationship fail.

Teresa, Carla's sister, has another point. She agrees the marriage will have a huge impact on Haley's life but she thinks Haley and Carla both have a negative view about the future. "It's possible this marriage will have a positive effect on Haley. Her mom will be happier, there will be another adult around to help things run smoothly, and there will be another income, so less stress over money," Teresa explained.

Sometimes it's easier to see the negatives. It takes more effort to see the positives, especially when you're scared, confused, or nervous. But when you can look at the positives, there is a much greater chance of things working out well.

So let's summarize the group's feedback:

1. You have a right to feel upset when you don't have control, but teens can't expect always to be asked for their opinion—it's just not going to happen!

2. If you want to improve things at home, you should discuss your feelings. Translation: *Talk* it out!

3. You should watch how you behave so you don't make things worse by acting out negative feelings. Read: Don't *act* out!

4. Look for the positives in your parent's marriage. Looking for only negatives can be a drag and makes it hard to improve things in your life.

What if it doesn't work . . . ?

If you find yourself in a situation that you really can't stand and can't change, start planning your future. Think about how you will be able to move out successfully. Concentrate on schoolwork so you can get a good job or go to college after you graduate high school. Work part-time and start saving money so you can be independent more quickly. In other words, take control of your life; don't rely on your parents to make you happy.

My mom says this new stepfamily will be great, but why will this family work when our first one didn't?

> *Danielle:* My mom will say *anything* to convince me everything is fine, but it's totally bogus. Our first family got messed up and so will this one.

We won't lie. Of course there's a chance your stepfamily won't be any more successful than your first family. And you know from experience that there's no guarantee. But having said that, there is reason to be optimistic that things will be different this time around. Your parent has had tons of experience in a relationship that didn't work. Your parent has probably figured out what he or she wants and doesn't want in a partner. So it's likely that your stepparent is a better match for your mom or dad than your other parent was. This alone is reason enough for things to work out between them. But there are other reasons, too. Sometimes parents separate because they met when they were young, and over time they grew apart and had less and less in common with each other. But now your mom or dad is older and more settled than the first time around. So your parent is less likely to change or drift apart from a new partner. Here's one more reason why your stepfamily is not doomed to fail: Your mom or dad loves you and is going to do his or her best not to give you another bad life experience. This means that your parent will try very hard to make the relationship and the new stepfamily work.

There are things that your parent, stepparent, and the kids (including you!) can do to increase the odds that things will work out. We got lots of suggestions from stepteens and made a list of the best ones. Make sure that your parent and stepparent read this chapter, too. Maybe they'll get some ideas that they haven't thought of yet.

StepSolutions

1. Have weekly family meetings to discuss everyone's concerns and complaints.

2. Remember that it can take a year or longer for a stepfamily to start to work.

3. Ask your parent not to make your stepparent the "bad guy" too much when it comes to discipline—it'll give you more time to develop a good relationship with your stepparent.

4. Respect each other's differences—you're all coming from very different backgrounds. This means adults respecting kids and kids respecting adults.

5. If you're too angry to talk without fighting, try writing a letter and giving it to the person you are mad at. Maybe you can talk after the letter has been read.

6. Don't jump to conclusions. Sometimes we misinterpret each other's actions and words. This is even more likely to happen in a family where people are just getting to know each other. If you're not sure why someone did or said something, ask before flying off the handle (adults too, please!).

7. Try not to gang up on each other—not adults against kids and not "my family" against "your family." If two people disagree, everyone else should butt out.

8. Don't feel like you have to do everything together, as a family. But don't do everything apart, either.

9. Recognize each other's efforts and say thank you, as often as you can (kids and adults).

10. If the family needs it, don't be embarrassed to get help. Counseling can do wonders to open up the lines of communication.

Some of these suggestions are easier to do than others. They have all worked really well in lots of stepfamilies. But *everyone has to do his or her part.* Each kid and adult has to make a real effort to work at the StepSolutions. It *can* be done; we know hundreds of families who have done it.

What if it doesn't work . . . ?

So, you're still really worried this family isn't
going to make it. There are two possible reasons
for your feelings. First, you may just have to give
yourself time to get used to the new family. As
everyone settles into their new routines and things
seem to be working, you will probably start to feel
more relaxed and secure. The second possibility is
that you are right in seeing real problems in your
parent's new relationship. If this is the case, it is likely
that your parent doesn't see them and probably
wouldn't respond well to your worries about the
marriage failing. You may have to protect yourself
from further hurt by remaining somewhat detached
from your stepparent and stepsiblings until you have
some sense of how things will turn out. This may
take months or, unfortunately, years. But it's better
to take things slowly, rather than be "burned" a
second time.

What should I call my stepparent?

> *Kristy:* Hey there ... uh, yeah ... what am I supposed to call you now that you're marrying my mom?

When Kristy first met her mother's boyfriend, Larry, she didn't call him anything because she hardly ever saw him. She would say hi and then head to her room to do homework or talk on the phone. Then he started to come over more often, and sometimes he would have dinner with Kristy and her mom. At first she spoke to him only when she caught his eye. Luckily Larry made lots of eye contact, so they got to talk quite a bit. After they became friendly, she became comfortable calling him Larry. When Kristy's mom told her she was going to marry Larry, Kristy wondered if she would have to call him Dad. She liked Larry, but he wasn't her father. She decided to keep calling him by his first name and see what happened. Actually, nothing happened. After he became her stepfather, Larry was still comfortable being called by his name. Her mom didn't mind it, either.

Some kids use a name that's not the same as what they call their parents, but it's close. For example, Kelly calls her stepfather Pops, and Justin calls his stepmother Ma and his mother Mom. Calling a stepparent by this kind of nickname is often a good compromise for teens who feel close to their stepparent but don't want to call them Mom or Dad. Some kids worry they will be expected to start calling their stepparent Mom or Dad right after the wedding. But most parents understand that it's a difficult transition for everyone, and that you will need time to figure out what you want to call your stepparent.

If you're really stuck about what to call your step, maybe your mom or dad will have some suggestions. At least they'll know you're concerned and will be even less likely to pressure you into calling your stepparent something that doesn't feel right. "Yeah, right," you're thinking, "I *might* just talk to my parents." We know something like this feels awkward, but isn't it better to feel awkward for a few minutes than for a few years? Sometimes pushing yourself, even if you're nervous, isn't such a bad idea. Another idea, if you can't come to a decision, is to talk to your good friends about it. Other teens, even those who aren't in stepfamilies, may have some really good ideas for you.

Occasionally, stepparents do get insulted if you don't call them Mom or Dad. For example, one stepmother said, "I feed her, shop with her, and do her laundry; the least she can do is call me Mom." If this happens, it may be a good idea to explain to your stepparent that you don't feel comfortable with "Mom" or "Dad" because those names are reserved for your real parents. Perhaps you can decide together on a name that feels comfortable for both of you. We *know* this type of talk isn't easy. You have to stand up for what you believe, but you have to do it in a way that is going to improve your stepfamily relationships. It's also a good idea to get your real parent in on this discussion in order to help your stepparent understand and not feel hurt.

Some kids have the opposite problem. Justin has a close relationship with his stepmother. He really wanted to call her Mom, but he knew it would hurt his mother's feelings. That's why he decided to compromise and call his stepmom "Ma." Justin was able to find a way to make himself and all of his parents comfortable.

Sometimes you start out calling a stepparent by one thing (their first name, for instance), but then over time, as the relationship changes, you naturally begin to call your stepparent something else. For example, Lindsay, whose mother had died, called her stepmother Joan for a few years. But then she thought it would be nice to have a "real mother" again so she asked Joan if she could call her Mom. Now she says "Mom" most of the time, although she still says "Joan" once in a while. Brent tried to call his stepfather Dad for a few months, but it didn't feel right. After he stopped trying to make the Dad thing work, he ended up calling his stepdad DJ—short for Dad John. Hey, it worked for them!

Most teens we spoke to felt the issue of what to

call your stepparent becomes less important after you have all been together for a while. They feel relationships are more important than names. Kristy, for example, has become close to her stepfather but still calls him Larry. And, of course, the stepmother we mentioned who did all the shopping and the laundry couldn't develop a close relationship with her stepdaughter simply by insisting on being called Mom. The bottom line is this: *It's important to figure out what you're going to call your stepparent, but it's more important to figure out how to develop a relationship with your step.*

What if it doesn't work . . . ?

Okay, it's been months and you still can't bring yourself to address your stepparent by a name . . . any name? At this point you just have to TAKE THE LEAP! This is *not* the most monumental decision you will ever have to make, and your step probably feels weird that you don't call him or her anything. We suggest using their first name. Take it from there or leave it at that!

Chapter Two
Who's in Charge?

As you probably know, the "who's the boss" battle between parents and teens has been going on forever. And the struggle becomes even harder when you add a stepparent to the mix. Now you're not sure whether it's your parent, stepparent, or you who should be in charge!

I don't want to take orders from my stepmother—she's not even my parent.

Greg: I swear, the next time my stepmother tells me to pick up my clothes or turn down the music, I am going to absolutely blow! She thinks she's my *real* mother or something!

OK, take this quiz . . .

1. When your real parent tells you to pick up your laundry, you:

> **a.** say, "Of course, Mother," then do it immediately.
>
> **b.** don't have to move from the computer, phone, or TV because your laundry is always neatly put away.
>
> **c.** complain under your breath that parents don't have a right to give orders, it's your stuff and you'll do it when you're ready.

2. When your real parent yells at you to "turn down that so-called music," you:

> **a.** ask if they would like to join you in listening because you think they may be able to learn to appreciate your music.
>
> **b.** apologize profusely and immediately turn it down.
>
> **c.** turn it from 10 to 9, then scream over the music that now you can hardly hear it.

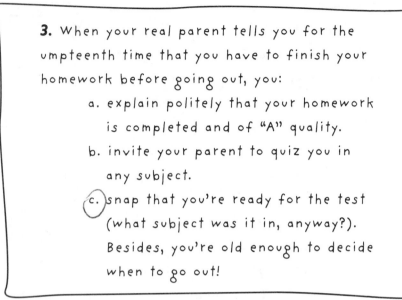

3. When your real parent tells you for the umpteenth time that you have to finish your homework before going out, you:

> a. explain politely that your homework is completed and of "A" quality.
> b. invite your parent to quiz you in any subject.
> c. snap that you're ready for the test (what subject was it in, anyway?). Besides, you're old enough to decide when to go out!

Did *you* answer **c** to all three questions? This quiz is a reminder that teenagers don't like to take orders from real or stepparents. Sometimes teens get furious when a stepparent gives an order, forgetting they would feel the same way if it were their real parent. Like your real parent, your step is just trying to keep the household sane. Not listening to your step might just be an excuse to get out of doing chores and homework! So if you have an otherwise good relationship with your stepparent, give him or her the same respect (or lack of respect!) you give your real parent.

While some stepparents realize it can take a long time for relationships to develop, others think they have to assert their "power" to become an instant parent. This is especially true for stepparents who don't have children because they haven't had experience relating to kids or teens. If you think that you have a power-hungry stepparent, here are some things you can do to improve things:

Put the Power in *Its* Proper Place

1. Talk to your parent calmly (*not* during a fight) about how you feel. Ask for help to improve things between you and your step.

2. Ask your parent if he or she could be the one to make and enforce rules until your relationship with your stepparent improves.

3. Explain to your stepparent (with your parent's help, if necessary) that you would like to develop a better relationship with him or her and that

once your relationship feels more comfortable
you will be less resistant to accepting discipline.

4. Be open to listening to your parent and
stepparent. It's possible that you are giving your
step a hard time because you're peeved that
your real mom or dad has been replaced. This
can be tough to admit, but in order to build a
relationship with your stepparent, you also have
to be willing to bend and change.

What if it doesn't work . . . ?

If your stepparent continues to boss you around
we suggest that you do your best to reduce conflict
by doing what your step asks and staying out of
his or her way. Clearly, your parent and stepparent
are in agreement, and if you continue to fight it,
they will both come down even harder on you.
This would be a good time to vent your feelings to
a friend, relative, school counselor, or someone else
you trust.

My mom always sides with my stepdad. She never sticks up for me, so I never get to do anything.

> *Craig:* The house rules used to be reasonable. But when my stepdad moved in, things changed. He doesn't want me out past ten P.M. even though my friends stay out until *at least* eleven. My mom won't stand up to him and pretends he's right.

We thought about Craig's dilemma and it occurred to us that this is really about the way Craig's mother has changed the way she makes rules since getting married. Do kids often feel their parents change (for the worse) when they remarry? To find out we conducted an informal poll of teens in stepfamilies. Almost everyone thought his or her parent changed at least a bit. Angie, who felt her father changed a lot, explained, "When we used to visit my dad, we had fun joking and being wild. Now that Margaret's here, he tells us to calm down and act our age. It's no fun anymore and he's always worried about how we behave around Margaret."

Shaun said his mother began to talk, act, and dress differently after she got married. She even dyed her hair. "I was freaked out when I came home from school and my mom's hair had gone from brown to blond. She and my stepdad just laughed at my shock, but I didn't think it was funny."

Like Angie and Shaun, you may also feel your mom or dad changed a lot after meeting someone new. But don't *you* dress, act, and talk differently when you start going out with someone? Of course you do! Well, new relationships affect adults as well as kids. Maybe Shaun's stepfather mentioned he'd like to see how Shaun's mom would look as a blond. Since she loves him and wants to make him happy, she decided to give it a try.

It can be weird to see your parent changing, and it may make you angry. But the real issue is whether the changes actually affect you. If they don't, like Shaun's mom changing her hair, it isn't fair to give your parent a hard time. After all, how many times have you worn clothes or done things your parents don't like? However, even if you can't really tell a parent what to do, you *can* and *should* talk to your mom or dad about your feelings. Perhaps they can explain why they changed and assure you that physical changes are superficial and won't affect your relationship with them.

The *real* dilemma is when the changes do affect you negatively. Take Craig's curfew. His stepfather's influence has caused his mom to change the rules, and Craig is really unhappy about this. Who can blame him . . . a ten o'clock curfew? Angie's situation isn't great, either. Her dad's worry about impressing Margaret has taken all the fun out of their visits. These teens have a legitimate gripe—they've had the rug pulled out from under them when it comes to predicting their parents.

But here's a news flash: You aren't going change your parents by yelling and screaming that they're being unfair. Parents are more likely to listen if you present a well-thought-out and rational case. So let's make a case. We consulted a team of lawyers who

told us we need an opening statement, some
supporting evidence, and a closing argument.
Here's a model you can follow:

Making Your Case

Opening Statement: Mom/Dad, I am confused
about changes at home. It seems that since you
married ___Hubby___ (fill in the blank) you are
different. I want to understand what the changes
mean. It's not easy getting used to living with
someone new and feeling that you've changed, too.
It also seems like the changes have to do with
___wife___ (stepparent) telling you what to do,
and that makes me angry.

Supporting Evidence: Here are some examples:
Do you remember when you used to ___have fun
time___ (fill in the blank with how things
were—be specific, it's really important!). Well,
now that you're married, you_____
_____
(fill in with specific changes).

Closing Argument: It would be great if things could go back to the way they were. But even if they can't, could you explain what's going on, especially the part about me feeling that _____ (stepparent) is making the rules and you're following along. I hope we can work things out because I don't like feeling so angry and fighting so much.

This strategy shows your parents that you can discuss important subjects without freaking out. It will give you credibility and your parents will be much more likely to listen. It can be used for any conversation with your parents, and it doesn't apply only to stepparent issues.

What if it doesn't work . . . ?

If you see the rules aren't changing no matter what you say or do, you are going to have to make the best of things. Maybe your parent believes the change is positive. And maybe it's part of the compromise necessary in any marriage. Perhaps you can sleep at a friend's house on some weekends and get a break from your household rules. You can also work at having fun with your parent in a different way. Try to make choices that do not result in you feeling sorry for yourself because it will only interfere with being able to make the best of things.

My dad shouldn't change the way we do things. After all, we were a family long before my stepmother came along. How do I get him to see it?

Missy: Since I'm the oldest, I was in charge when my dad was out. But after he married Mary, he let her be the boss. She doesn't really know my sisters or me, and we were doing fine without her.

Missy feels she had an important job taking care of her sisters, which was suddenly given to Mary, her stepmother. She is concerned that Mary won't do as good a job, since she doesn't know the girls the way

Missy does. Also, she doesn't think her dad really appreciates her for taking on a mothering role with her sisters. We discussed these thoughts with Missy.

We told Missy that she had a big job taking care of her sisters and she admitted that she didn't like it that much because it kept her from hanging out on the phone or going on-line until her dad came home. A part of her was even relieved to give up her responsibility.

We suggested to Missy that perhaps her dad realized she didn't really enjoy the responsibility of taking care of her sisters, and that's why he encouraged Mary to take over. Missy understood this point, but still somehow felt as if she had been replaced. In a way she had been replaced. But the job of mothering her sisters should have been only temporary anyway. She needed to have her own life.

When we reminded Missy that it would be nice to be able to spend more time with her friends, she agreed. But at the same time it was difficult for her to give up the control and decision-making. She also couldn't help wondering if her dad thought that

she hadn't been doing a good enough job with
her sisters.

We told Missy that no one was saying she wasn't
good enough to take care of her sisters. And that
in fact, it sounded like she had done a terrific job
with her sisters. We suggested that the real problem
may be that she is angry with her father for being
unappreciative and for making her feel like she is
not needed anymore. The way for her to fix this
problem is for Missy to talk to her dad.

Missy realized she was angry and upset because
her dad and Mary didn't appreciate what she'd
done. They made big changes without even talking
to her.

*"Yes, and it's understandable you're
upset," we said. "Let's take it another step.
You've admitted that being in charge was a
drag, right?"*

"Yeah, so?"

"You can't give up the responsibility and still expect your dad to do things your way. It's not fair to Mary. Besides, you're not the parent. It's hard to admit, but Mary is an adult. If your dad trusts her, you'll need to learn to trust her, too."

"I feel that she invaded our family, and instantly wants to be the mother. Things were going along fine before she came along."

We pointed out to Missy that part of her difficulty with Mary was about adjusting to having someone new in the family, and not just about who would take care of Missy's sisters. But we reminded her that in new stepfamilies it's just as hard for the new person. A new stepmom has to really work at fitting into the family and this can be especially tough if she's not even sure everyone in the family wants her.

Missy agreed but she wanted suggestions for making things less stressful at home. Our suggestions may help you as well: It's all about TALKING! Explain to your parent that you feel replaced, hurt, and angry and tell him or her it's hard to have a new person in the house. *But* you have to come clean about feeling relieved to give up the responsibility. It's only fair that your parent have the whole picture. If you can be open and respectful, your parent will be more sensitive to how you are affected by the changes. Also you and your stepparent should sit down together. Remember this is tough for him or her, too, but it will give both of you a chance to understand each other.

What if it doesn't work . . . ?

Sometimes adults aren't as open to kids' concerns as you would like them to be. But even if sharing your feelings doesn't work, you should still admit that having a stepparent accept responsibility gives you freedom. So use the situation to your advantage. Also, writing in a diary, talking to friends, or even talking to a counselor can help when you're especially angry or upset.

What should I do if my parent tells me one thing, and my stepparent says something else?

> ***Deena:*** My mother said I don't have to go to a boring family picnic. But then my stepdad said I have to go. I *always* get stuck in the middle, and I don't want to upset either of them. Sometimes they even end up fighting with each other.

Deena brought this problem to a stepteen chat session, so we decided to give the group our quick True/False "Kid in the Middle" Quiz. Why don't you take the quiz, too? We'll discuss Deena's responses and figure out a way to help her.

True/False Kid in the Middle Quiz

Circle the correct answer.

1. You should always listen to your real parent over your stepparent.   Ⓣ **F**

2. You should always listen to your   T   (F)
stepparent over your real parent.

3. When your parent and stepparent   (T)   F
disagree, you can choose whom you
want to listen to.

4. When your parent and stepparent   (T)   F
argue, you should side with the one
who is most upset.

5. If your parents are arguing about you,   (T)   F
it means it's somehow your fault.

6. Parents should not argue in front of kids. (T)   F

7. If one parent says no to something you   (T)   F
want, it's okay to ask the other parent to
see if that parent says yes.

8. Parents should try to agree on important   T   (F)
issues before giving you a response.

Correct Responses: (1.) F, (2.) F, (3.) F, (4.) F, (5.) F, (6.) T, (7.) F, (8.) T
Deena's Responses: (1.) F, (2.) F, (3.) F, (4.) T, (5.) T, (6.) F, (7.) F, (8.) F
(Underlined responses are incorrect.)

The group's impressions of Deena's quiz:

Randi: "Deena thinks it's her responsibility to make sure her parents don't fight, but it isn't."

Marc: "She also thinks if the fight is about her, it's her fault. But adults are responsible for their own fights, no matter what they're fighting about!"

Loren: "Parents should not fight in front of their kids. Also, Deena's mom should've checked with her stepdad before saying it was okay to skip the picnic. Then Deena wouldn't have ended up in the middle."

These teens have excellent insight into Deena's dilemma. We just want to add that there are also many non-stepfamilies in which kids wind up in the middle of parental arguments. Indeed, this seems to be less about stepparenting and more about parenting in general. In fact, why don't you consider showing this next section to your parents to open up a discussion.

✖ Step and "real" parents should realize that kids should not be put in a position where they have to choose one or the other parent.

✖ Parents should stand united in the way they make decisions about their kids. They should talk to each other before giving kids an answer about an important issue.

✖ If parents disagree strongly with each other, they should do so privately so kids are not subjected to their fighting. This is particularly true in stepfamilies where there was a divorce because kids have usually experienced lots of parental fighting before, during, and after the divorce. They are sensitive and get nervous when they hear their parent and stepparent arguing.

✖ Now this is the most important part: No matter what parents are fighting about, it is never, ever the kids' fault. It is also *not* the responsibility of kids to stop them from arguing.

✖ *But* it is a kid's responsibility to make sure not to play parents against each other. If one says no, it isn't right to ask the other, hoping for a yes.

What if it doesn't work . . . ?

What can you do if your parents don't take responsibility for the way they act? It's tricky, but you have to separate yourself and stay out of their arguments. For example, when Marc's parents disagree, he says, "You guys figure it out, then let me know afterwards." He realizes there's nothing he can do and it's not his fault. If the arguing really stresses you out, talk to someone, like a close friend or relative. It's always easier to deal with problems when you have some support.

I hate going to my dad's house since he got married because there are tons more rules. What can I do?

Megan: My dad has never been the easiest person to deal with, but now things are impossible. Since he married Katherine, you can't move without breaking a rule. I don't even want to visit every other weekend as scheduled.

It's important to know what Megan meant when she said her dad has never been the easiest person. Can you figure out why?

Is it because . . .

A) Maybe Megan is using her dad's marriage as an excuse not to visit, since she isn't close to him.

B) Perhaps her dad has always been difficult, and being a stickler about rules is just an example of that.

C) It may just seem to Megan that he has too many rules because she generally has a hard time with him.

D) All of the above.

Did you get the correct answer, (D) All of the above?

The Real Problem

It's not unusual for teens to blame their stepparents for every problem from failing a bio test ("She was watching TV so I couldn't study") to not being asked out by a crush ("She answered the phone when he called"). But let's face it, not everything is your stepparent's fault. In fact, there are many problems (maybe even most) that have nothing to do with your stepparent!

When we asked Megan to consider the four options, she acknowledged she really didn't *want* to visit her dad.

"He makes new rules as he goes along," she explained. "I think it's worse since Katherine, but it's always been that way, even before my parents separated."

It was evident that Megan's problem was really with her father, more so than with her stepmother. Megan realized that it was easy to blame everything on Katherine because she *could* be very annoying, but actually her dad and she had never seen eye to eye. As she said,

"He doesn't understand that rules aren't going to make me obey him. Instead of talking, he yells, gives orders, and complains. Katherine is exactly the same way."

Megan asked us what she should do. Fortunately we've talked with several kids who have handled similar situations. We put their suggestions together with our own.

Finding a Solution

1. Look at your relationship with your parents realistically—maybe you've always had certain problems with them.

2. Don't automatically blame your stepparent or assume he or she will make things worse.

3. If you sense your stepparent can be an ally, talk to your step openly to help you with your parent problems.

4. Realize that your parent may make more rules because someone else (your step) is supporting the family now.

5. If things get bad, talk to your parent and stepparent (calmly!). Help them realize you're having a hard time with too many rules.

What if it doesn't work . . . ?

Life isn't always fair, and wishing things were different won't make it so. Sometimes you need to manage by adjusting to the situation. It is possible that your stepparent really is fueling the negative vibes. In this case, you need to consider ways to survive the relationship as well as possible for as long as you have to. For example, spend as little time as you need to with your parents. Keep yourself busy, stay out of the way, and try hard not to break any of the big rules. Spend time with your friends or even in your room. (You may get more homework done!) If your problem is with a parent whom you visit, you can do the same, and if things are really bad, consider limiting your visits. *But*, before trying these "avoidance" techniques, be sure your complaints are fair. If you aren't sure, speak with someone objective whom you trust—don't assume your best friend is objective. Don't forget to try the communication methods *first* and resort to avoidance only if nothing else works.

Chapter Three
Stepsiblings and New Babies

You've heard of "sibling rivalry," right? Well, what about stepsibling rivalry? And what about that weird feeling you get when your parent and stepparent tell you they're having a baby? As you can imagine, having stepsiblings and new babies can make things even more complicated than just having a stepparent.

My dad disciplines me much more strictly than my stepmother's kids.

Donna: Last night, I was fifteen minutes late for curfew, and my dad grounded me for two weeks. But when my stepsister was an hour late, he just reminded her of curfew. He obviously treats us totally differently.

We took Donna's question to an expert—Greg, father of three and stepfather of two kids. Greg met with Donna and us. We wondered what he thought about Donna's situation.

"Here's a possible explanation," began Greg. "When I first became a stepfather, it was awkward for me to discipline my stepkids. They resented it—and me—so I had to leave the discipline to Erica, their mom. The only problem was that her idea of discipline and mine were different. She believed teenagers need strict rules, and I remember how much I hated that when I was a kid, so I tried to be more relaxed with my kids."

Greg explained that there was a lot fighting in his new family because he and Erica couldn't agree. She disciplined her kids her way and he did the same with his. The kids argued constantly with both of them and with each other.

We explained to Greg and Donna that this type of arguing is not unusual in newly formed stepfamilies. And sometimes it seems extremely difficult to work things out. Greg explained how he and Erica broke down the communication barriers.

"We hashed the whole thing out at a family meeting. In the end, we agreed everyone would be treated equally, somewhere between my way and Erica's. Neither Erica nor I was thrilled about giving up our way." We reminded everyone that the reality of a stepfamily is that you *always* have to compromise. It's impossible for two families to come together and not change. We asked Greg why it felt awkward to discipline his stepchildren.

"When I disciplined my own kids, I only had to worry whether they were going to listen to me. With my stepkids, I worried that my discipline would make them hate me. Or that they'd compare me negatively to their father. I was afraid that if I were too strict they'd reject me, which would be bad for the family and for my marriage. So I went lighter on them than on my own kids."

Role-play Play-by-play

We suggested that Greg and Donna role-play a conversation of a daughter working out an issue with her father.

Donna agreed to start.

"Dad, there's something happening that's really bothering me. Can we talk about it?"

"Sure, Donna, what's the problem?"

"Well, it seems like you treat Erica's kids better than you treat us, and it's causing problems among the kids."

By saying "it seems like" Donna isn't accusing her dad. Also, by saying "it's causing problems among the kids" too, she's showing her dad it's not just about typical fighting between parents and teens.

"Do you have some examples to help me understand?"

Parents are big on examples, so you should always be ready with some. It also makes your point much stronger.

"Remember when I missed curfew I was grounded, but when Sue missed curfew you didn't even yell at her."

Stay calm and make a rational case.

"I see your point. I'll think about it and talk to Erica. Maybe we can change things a bit."

We stopped the role-play and encouraged Donna to use these skills with her parents.

If, like Donna, you feel your parent is treating you and your stepsibs differently, you should first consider that it's not simple to discipline someone else's kids. So give your parent or stepparent a break. Then talk about what's bothering you. Hopefully, they will realize what's happening and make some changes.

What if it doesn't work . . . ?

The truth is, parents don't always see things the way their kids do. It's even possible they will think you're making excuses for not living by the house rules. What should you do now? One approach is to try to get all the kids in the family together to talk to your parents. It's likely that your stepsibs are also uncomfortable, even if they're being treated better. After all, tension among stepsiblings is no fun for anyone. You could also discuss the issue with your stepparent. He or she may be able to get through to your parent better than you could. If nothing works, you're just going to have to deal with it. Keep in mind that being a stepparent is tough, and your parent may not be able to do everything perfectly.

My stepbrother won't stay out of my stuff, no matter how many times I ask. It's driving me crazy!

> *Patrick:* My younger stepbrother always borrows my CDs, clothes, and other cool stuff without permission. I've asked him not to, but he won't stop.

Younger siblings (step or otherwise) always want to get into your stuff. In fact, there's a secret list of commandments all younger siblings know, designed to drive their teenage sisters and brothers crazy. We'll share them with you, right here, right now. (Just don't take them seriously!)

How to Successfully Sneak a Teenager's Stuff

1. Inspect your teenage sibling's stuff regularly to see if there's anything new.

2. If you see something you like, don't ask first, just borrow it. If you ask, you'll be rejected anyway.

3. When asked whether you took it, always say no, even if you did. You'll get yelled at anyway.

4. You don't have to return things in good condition.

5. In fact, you don't have to return them at all.

6. If teenagers come looking for their stuff, scream, "You can't come in without permission." It's what they always say to *you*, right?

7. If they threaten to tell, remind them of the mean things they do to you.

8. If your sibling does tell, start crying, "He *never* shares and his stuff is so awesome. I'm really sorry. I'll never do it again"

9. Don't worry about getting in trouble; by next week all will be forgotten and you will be able to begin borrowing again.

10. The only way to learn what it's like to be a teenager is to borrow a teenager's stuff and practice.

So, now you know why younger kids take your stuff. They admire you, are curious about being a teenager, and want to feel what it's like to be using your stuff. They figure (and rightly so) that you won't let them borrow it, so they just take it. They also figure it's a good way to get attention from you, even if it means fighting. All they really want is to be like you and be with you. This is especially true if your stepsib is the same sex as you. For example, a little girl will be thrilled to use a teenage girl's clothes, makeup, hair stuff, and nail polish. You may not feel like one, but you are a role model.

The Teen Commandments for Dealing with Younger Stepsiblings

1. Ask your stepsib (nicely!) to speak to you before taking your things. And ask parents to enforce this.

2. Tell your stepsib (this is the hard part) that *if* they ask you nicely to borrow something that you will try not to say no. Mean what you say!

3. When you lend something, remind your stepsib that you expect it back in good condition. Here's a line that works: "I'm letting you borrow this because I trust you. So please be careful with my stuff."

4. If you're not sure you can trust your stepsib, try to compromise. For example, invite him to your room to listen to a CD or offer to give her a manicure with your nail polish. This will give your stepsib a chance to try your stuff and spend time with you, which is exactly the point.

5. If something borrowed gets ruined, don't go ballistic. Try explaining that you want to be able to lend stuff, but you won't if your stepsib wrecks it. Lay on the guilt trip—say that you trusted him or her, and that you want things to work out between the two of you. That kind of thing. You'll get further this way than by yelling and whining to parents.

6. If there are *several* disasters, then speak to a parent. Don't do it as a nagging, complaining teenager! Explain that you've tried to lend your stuff freely, but it hasn't been treated well or hasn't been returned. At this point, ask for a parent's help.

7. And don't forget that *you* were once an irresponsible kid who didn't know how to treat other people's stuff.

Okay, let's recap. The kid takes your stuff because he or she admires you and wants to be like you. Hard to believe, but it's the truth! The trick is to give some access to your stuff and make it understood that it's a matter of trust between you. As long as he or she is respectful of your things and returns them, you should continue to lend them. If it doesn't work out, try to share your stuff with your supervision. If necessary, get a parent to help you out. That's it!

What if it doesn't work . . . ?

It's possible that your stepsib may not respect your belongings and privacy no matter what you do. You may also have parents who aren't good at enforcing privacy rules or who don't think privacy is a big deal. In this case, don't leave your things lying around where they can be taken easily—this may mean tidying up your room once in a while! If necessary, hide them. When the problem is very serious, you should lock up important things. For example, put your CDs in a drawer or closet you can lock. You can even ask your parents if you can lock your bedroom door while you're out. But don't be surprised if they say no. Parents generally aren't thrilled with locked bedrooms, even if you're not inside. And by all means, make it clear to stepsibs that it will be difficult for you to establish a good relationship with them if you don't feel they respect you.

My stepmother obviously favors her own children. Is this unfair?

Nancy: I like my stepmother and her kids. But I feel she favors them, feels sorry for them, and treats them much more patiently. But she *is* their mother so maybe I'm overreacting.

Nancy shared these concerns with a few stepteens during an after-school get-together. Of course, everyone had a different point of view.

Jake felt she was lucky that she even liked her steps. He had been in a stepfamily for three years and his family still didn't get along. Beth agreed with Nancy. "My stepdad has two kids and sometimes I wish he were my real dad, too," she said. "He's nicer to me than my own father, and I'm jealous of his kids."

It's not unusual for a stepkid to wish he or she had a closer relationship with a stepparent and even to be jealous of stepsibs. But it's important not to allow the jealousy to interfere with your relationships because then, instead of things growing closer over time, you could find yourself becoming more distant from your stepfamily.

Harry, another stepteen, also felt he was less favored by his stepparent. "My stepfather definitely pays more attention to his kids—their homework, driving them around; a lot more than he does for me," he said. When Nancy asked him if he asked his stepdad for help, he told her he didn't because his mom does a lot for him. "Maybe he thinks you don't *want* his help because you never ask," Nancy said. "He may feel that *you* don't want a relationship with *him*. My stepmom does stuff for me. I'm not complaining. But she is more patient with her kids. Maybe it is because their dad died about four years ago."

When a parent dies, parents and children often grieve for a long time, even after the other parent remarries. These feelings can affect the way family members treat each other. For example, Nancy's stepmother is very sensitive to not upsetting her children. She also tries to be both mom and dad to them. Despite being embarrassed about her jealousy, Nancy agreed to talk to her stepmom about her feelings. Although she felt nervous about the conversation, she realized it would only make things worse if she kept her feelings hidden and became more and more upset.

What if it doesn't work . . . ?

Once in a while, kids live in a real Cinderella situation where their stepparent treats them much worse than his or her own kids. If your stepparent treats you badly, no matter how much you try to negotiate change, the first thing to do is discuss your concerns with the parent you're living with. If this doesn't work, speak to another adult with whom you feel close (other parent, aunt, uncle, grandparent, school counselor, etc.). If the situation is unbearable, you may have to consider living elsewhere for a time. If it's not unbearable, try to stay as uninvolved with your stepparent as you can so you don't become a target. You also need to consider honestly whether you're doing anything to contribute to your stepparent's negative feelings. If you don't live with this stepparent, you can explain your concerns to your parent or try to plan visits that don't include your stepparent.

I worry that my stepfather and his kids are more important to my mom than I am.

> **Tyrone:** My mom spends so much time with my stepdad and his kids, it doesn't seem like she cares about me anymore.

After talking to Tyrone we discovered that his relationship with his mom had been fine until she remarried. Then Tyrone felt pushed right out of the picture. No wonder he's upset!

Do you have Tyrone's problem? Take this quiz to find out.

Where Do I Fit Now That There's a New Family?

1. Did you and your parent have a close   **Y   N**
relationship before the stepfamily? Are you
close now?

2. Did you get enough attention from your   Ⓨ **N**
     mom or dad back then? What about now?

3. Were your needs a priority before?   **Y** Ⓝ
     Are they a priority now?

4. Does your mom or dad suddenly feel   Ⓨ **N**
     you're being too demanding?

It's important to answer honestly. If your needs
were *never* met, then you can't blame the new
marriage for your parent not making you a priority
now. However, seeing your mom or dad treat your
steps better than you might make it feel worse. You
will need to talk to your parent, a counselor, relative,
or other trusted adult to help you figure out how to
improve things between you and your parent, in and
out of your stepfamily.

When Tyrone took this quiz, all his responses
before the stepfamily were yes! His relationship
with his mother used to be close, and she spent lots
of time helping him with homework, driving him

around, and talking to him. When she remarried, it came as a shock to Tyrone that she began to invest so much time in his stepdad and stepsiblings. So what's going on here?

Actually, there's a fairly simple answer. Tyrone's mother *is* investing a lot of emotional energy in her new marriage, and she does want to develop a good stepparenting relationship with her stepchildren. This is a legitimate concern because his mother wants this marriage to work out. So while it may seem to Tyrone that he is getting the short end of the stick, his mother is actually doing this as much for him as for herself. She doesn't want Tyrone to have to deal with another painful divorce.

It is not easy for a bunch of people to suddenly come together as a new family, and it takes lots of work to do it successfully. Tyrone's mom is probably working overtime to make things run smoothly with the steps, and since his relationship with his mom was secure, he probably has been put on the back burner for a while.

In a way, it's a compliment that Tyrone's mom is

secure enough in her relationship with him to feel it can withstand a period of less attention. Maybe Tyrone's mom needs his support while the new family relationships are developing. The danger is if a lack of attention and caring becomes routine. This is not a good thing!

Tyrone was really angry with his mom and resentful of his stepfamily. And Tyrone thought that his mom could read his mind—he never told her how he felt! He screamed, fought, and argued with her and his steps about all kinds of things, but never once told his mom how he felt their relationship had changed over the last few months or how sad he felt about it. We encouraged Tyrone to talk to her. When he did, he was surprised to find out that his mom didn't even realize she was treating him differently.

It stands to reason that if there was a decent relationship before steps came on the scene, it should be able to be repaired with some communication and effort on everyone's part. We said it before, but it's worth repeating: If a

relationship was iffy before the steps, don't expect
it to suddenly get better now, and don't blame
the stepfamily.

What if it doesn't work . . . ?

What if your parent, unlike Tyrone's mom, isn't
open to hearing your concerns? First, you need
to recognize that for things to have changed so
drastically, your parent must be having some difficulty
with the steps. This could be making him or her
work overtime on these relationships. For example,
perhaps the stepchildren are hard to deal with, or
maybe the marriage requires extra effort to work
out some kinks. Your complaining may be perceived
as just one more problem. Rather than sinking into
self-pity, look for some support elsewhere to get
you through a hard time.

Your friends will definitely provide a sympathetic
ear. You can also speak to a trusted adult who knows
your parent. They may be able to help you by talking
to your mom or dad for you, or by suggesting other
ways for you to approach your parent. Keep in mind

that this isn't about you. It's about how your parent is (or isn't) coping with big life changes. So don't wait around for things to improve—make them better yourself. You may need to find help with schoolwork at school, to get rides with friends, and to seek out time and attention from other adults. But don't stop trying to talk to your mom or dad—he or she may eventually see your point.

I'm jealous because my dad's stepkids get to spend more time with him than I do.

> *Katie:* I missed a cool snowboarding trip with my dad because it wasn't my weekend with him. *And*, since his stepkids live with him, they got to go. It's so unfair that they're with him more than I am.

The Feelings

- You wish you had more time with your dad.
- You're jealous that your stepsibs get more time with him than you do.

- Does he *have* to do the really *fun* things when you're not around?
- You feel left out of his new family because you're not always there.

The Facts

- Your parents are divorced and your dad is remarried.
- You live with your mom and visit your dad every other weekend.
- Your dad plans activities for his stepchildren during the times you're not there.
- You miss out on things when it's not your weekend.
- You do fun things that don't include him because he's not always around.

The Fix

It's no mystery that you're upset because you don't get to see your dad more often, and it's even more understandable that you're jealous of your stepsibs. But here are some things you can do to improve your situation:

1. Accept that divorce means you have to live with one parent. Your parents tried to make the best choice for everyone. (If you're not happy with your current living situation, check out chapter 5.)

2. Realize that everyone's busy lives (and especially yours!) make it difficult for you to see your dad more often.

3. If you do want to see him (and your steps) more often, *tell him!* He can't read your mind. Then, make a plan to go there an extra weekend a month and an extra holiday here and there. Or maybe he can pick you up for dinner more often.

4. Phone calls and e-mail count, too. So use technology to stay in touch as much as possible.

5. Make sure your dad knows about all of your sporting events, concerts, plays, etc., so he can plan to attend. Don't count on your mom to tell him. (One reason that they got divorced was probably because they didn't communicate well in the first place.)

6. If you want your dad to save really excellent activities for the times you're visiting, make sure he knows. Ask him to talk to you before planning big events.

7. Don't assume your visiting schedule is set in stone. Teenagers generally have as much flexibility as they want to visit their parents, so take advantage of it.

8. Try to be understanding of your stepsibs. After all, they've had some bad experiences, like divorce, too. You probably have more in common than you realize. Try to *relate* rather than *resent*.

9. Talk to your dad and stepmom about ways to make you feel more involved in their new family. They can help only if they know how you feel.

10. Acknowledge that you sometimes do fun things that don't include your dad. It's just part of growing up. Independence means you don't always share experiences with your parents, whether they're divorced or not.

What if it doesn't work . . . ?

If you just can't get that jealous feeling to go away, you need to share it with someone who can help you. You may be able to talk to your mom, but she's probably not the most objective person on this particular subject. But guess what? There are people trained to help teens work out really difficult feelings like jealousy and anger—guidance counselors, therapists, psychologists, and social workers, just to name a few. You can start by going to your school counselor to talk or just to get some ideas where to go next. You can also tell your mom and dad that you'd like to speak to someone to work out some private issues. It's important not to ignore your feelings because jealousy can fester and become a real problem for you later on. Besides, you'll feel so much better if you unload some of the negative feelings.

My mother and stepfather are having a baby. Will they forget about me?

> **Debra:** I'm not sure how I feel about having a new sister or brother, but I am worried they'll love the baby more—I mean, it's my stepdad's *real* kid and I'm not.

Debra's concern is very common among kids whose parent and stepparent have a new baby, and we wondered whether this was something she thought about a lot. She offered to read the page from her diary where she wrote about it.

Dear Diary,

I couldn't believe it when my parents divorced, and just when I got used to it my mom remarried. Okay, I'm sorta used to that, and *now* they tell me they're having a baby! The main problem is that this baby will be living with *both* its real parents while I only have my mom—I do love my stepdad but he's not my *real* dad. So this lucky baby won't have to deal with all the fighting, crying, divorce, and visiting weekends. And then, when I visit my real dad they will be alone with the baby, just like a little family without me. Maybe they won't *want* me to come back. Maybe I'll have to stay at my dad's house all the time because they want to be alone with the baby. And I also bet my stepdad won't love me as much as he loves the baby because the baby is *really* his and I'm not. Well, diary, I can already tell it's going to be rough. I am kinda excited about having a little sister or brother, but what if the baby is so cute they forget about me?

Debra certainly has some legitimate concerns. There is also another point of view. We spoke to another teen, Harry, who is fourteen and was once a new baby born into a stepfamily. We thought it would be helpful for Debra to hear from Harry what it's like from the other side.

"I really like having a big sister," explained Harry. "Her name's Emily—and it doesn't matter that we've got different moms, we're still brother and sister all the way! The only thing I don't like is that Emily lives with her mom and visits us on weekends. I wish she lived with us all the time because I miss her and we always have to say goodbye.

"Debra, you and your baby are lucky you'll live together because it's great to have a sister. My dad loves us both equally even though he's married to my mom and not Emily's. The way he explains it is that he fell out of love with her mom. But he'll always love Emily because she's his daughter. I'm sure your mom will love you after she has the baby. My mom also loves Emily a lot. She tells us she's lucky she had Emily as a stepdaughter. That experience taught her how to be a good mom before I was born. Debra, I bet your stepdad will still love you after your baby is born and he will be happy that the baby has a big sister."

A Few More New-Baby Pointers

☞ Ask your mom or dad to count you in on decisions and preparations for the baby so you don't feel left out.

☞ Talk to your parents about your feelings—they can address your concerns only if they know about them.

☞ Give your parent and stepparent a chance to get used to having a baby; they may need *your* support and help.

☞ It will probably take a couple of months after the baby is born for things to get back to normal. Babies can be *very* exhausting. Just ask your parent what you were like!

☞ Instead of feeling sorry for yourself, pitch in and help! The best way to be a great big brother or sister is to really spend time with the baby. Maybe you can even make a little money baby-sitting for your new sib on Saturday nights!

What if it doesn't work . . . ?

Although it hardly ever happens, some parents

get so wrapped up in the new baby they seem to forget about their older children. If you feel this is really happening, the first thing to do is *talk to your parents* so they become aware that you are feeling hurt. Hopefully, this will encourage them to change things. If it doesn't work, you will need to find other ways to tell them how you feel. Try writing a letter or sending an e-mail. Make sure they realize you love the baby but you feel you've been pushed to the side. It may also help to tell them that you are becoming resentful of your sibling because you're jealous of all the attention he or she gets, and you don't feel you get enough. You should also talk to other people because talking about feelings is much better than keeping them stuck inside you. Besides, other people—adults and your buds—can give you some good suggestions for how to handle things.

Chapter Four
Always Stuck in the Middle

Have you ever felt like you're in the middle of a sandwich? Well, being in a stepfamily can be just like that. Sometimes you feel stuck between your parent and stepparent, and if your parents are divorced, you can feel caught between them, too.

My mom criticizes my stepmother, and my dad gets upset if I don't take his side against my stepfather. I'm caught in the middle because I don't want to hurt anyone's feelings.

Josh: Even though they seem happily remarried, both of my parents are still bitter. It's not enough that I love them; they each want me to hate the other's spouse. When will they get over it and let me enjoy my new life?

Unfortunately, when parents divorce they don't always get over the fighting, anger, and sadness from the divorce. They may still be fighting about huge issues like custody, money, and the stuff they have to divide up. Like Josh said, they're often really bitter. In fact, your parents may have gotten divorced *years ago* and all the legal issues may have been settled, and still they feel like this. It's not so different from you having a huge falling-out with your best friend, whom you've known since you were a baby. You'd be bitter, too. Now, how would you feel if your ex-friend suddenly got a new best friend? Pretty bad, right? That's how your parents feel, too. Even if they *wanted* the divorce and don't want to be together, they still seem to get upset, angry, and even jealous if the other decides to remarry. *But*, there is one big difference between you and your parents: They are adults with kids, and you're not. So even though they're entitled to feel really bad, it's not okay for them to put you in the middle.

The problem is some parents don't realize what they're doing. Others do realize, but jealousy and bitterness rule their decision-making, and you suffer. If you find yourself in this situation, you're not alone. And you're going to have to set major boundaries on what you're willing to deal with in order to stop your parents from using you as a messenger, therapist, or pawn against one another.

Margaret and Jill, sisters who decided they just couldn't take it anymore, came up with a set of limit-setting rules for themselves. Since they swear by it, we gave it to Josh to try for a month. His response was equally positive: "Wow, this is totally awesome! I never realized how much control I could have. I don't have to let my parents use me to get to each other." With these kinds of rave reviews, we've included Margaret and Jill's rules. We hope they help you, too.

The Basics of Boundaries

I. Tell your parents and stepparents very clearly that *you do not want them ever to bad-mouth the other parent, other stepparent, or stepkids to you.*

2. Ask your parents not to talk to you about "money problems" concerning your other parents (e.g., "Ask your father to buy you new sneakers!" or "Your mother thinks I should give her everything and live on nothing myself").

3. If one parent (or stepparent) starts to speak negatively about the other one, or about uncomfortable money issues, stop them immediately. If they don't stop, *walk away without hesitation.*

4. Don't tell one parent (or stepparent or stepkids) negative things that the other parent has said. You'll become part of the problem by making things worse.

5. Don't allow yourself to be sucked into taking sides. If one parent demands your allegiance against the other, remind yourself the request is unreasonable.

6. Maintain your integrity. Do not allow a parent to *bribe* you (money, CDs, concert tickets, clothes) to take a particular side. Relationships are far more important than stuff!

7. Refuse to deliver messages (good or bad) from one parent to another. Parents tend to become angry with the messenger if they don't like the news.

8. Refuse to be a "shoulder to cry on" or a "good listener" for a parent who is unloading about your other parent. It's not your role, and it's wrong for your parent to put you in that position. If your parent doesn't get this, you need to.

9. Do not feel guilty. You are entitled to a good relationship with both your parents and any stepfamily members. It's completely inappropriate for one parent to sabotage these relationships by expecting you to play favorites or to take sides.

10. If you see a parent using a younger sib to get
to the other parent, don't ignore it. Teach your
brother or sister how to stand up to your parent
and support him or her in doing it.

What if it doesn't work . . . ?

If, no matter what you do, your parent won't
stop bad-mouthing the other side, you are going to
have to accept that. You will have to recognize the
burden is on you not to participate in this behavior.
Focus, instead, on maintaining and developing
relationships with your other parent and stepfamily.
If you live with the offending parent, and if it is an
option, you may consider moving in with your other
parent to avoid dealing with the "parent bashing" on
a regular basis. If both parents are guilty, you'll just
have to work at maintaining your boundaries. After
all, you can only be responsible for yourself!

I feel guilty having fun with my father and stepmother because my mom always quizzes me about it. It makes me uncomfortable. How do I get her to stop?

> **Yolanda:** When I come from visiting my dad and his wife, my mom wants to know every detail of what we did. I think she wants to see if I have more fun with them than with her. Sometimes I lie to her because I *do* have a good time with them.

When we asked Yolanda for the details, she told us this story.

"I don't usually tell my mom about the fun things I do there because I don't want her to be jealous. But one time I was so aggravated, I told her that Rosalie, my stepmom, took me shopping for fabulous, expensive clothes. Of course it was all a lie. The next day my mom asked if I wanted to go shopping (I usually have to beg). We went to the mall and she got me everything I wanted. I was so psyched, and it just cracked me up that she was doing it to compete with my stepmother! I did the same thing the next weekend with CDs, and she went out the next day and got me a bunch of the CDs I'd been dying for! My luck ran out when she mentioned to my dad that he'd been generous with me lately. Of course, he didn't know what she was talking about. Was she mad! But she was also really embarrassed about having bought me stuff just to show up my stepmom."

Looking at Yolanda's story, it seems there are two sets of issues, hers and her mother's. You may be dealing with similar issues, so let's take a look at both and figure out how to resolve the problem.

Your Parent's Problem

Parents often feel that they have to compete with a stepparent you like, even if that isn't how you feel. They feel threatened and jealous of the time you spend with your other parent and stepfamily. Some parents have told us they don't like feeling this way but they can't stop themselves. Their behavior, prompted by jealousy and a worry that they will lose you to "the other side," sometimes seems crazy. And sometimes it drives you crazy. However, you know the feelings you've had that your mom or dad will love the stepkids more than you. Well, it's the same thing. Your mom or dad worries that you'll love the stepparent more.

Your Problem

You're stuck in the middle. You want to enjoy being with your parent and stepfamily, but you don't want your other parent to be upset or to make you feel guilty. And although Yolanda's story was funny, the issues it represents are quite serious. By lying to her mother, Yolanda just made the situation worse. It's hard enough already without more confusion. So what are your choices? You can pretend you don't have a good time and feel guilty about lying (because you really did have fun). Or you don't lie, but you have to deal with your parent "punishing" you by sulking, yelling, or ignoring you when you return from the visit.

The Jealous-Parent Fix

Step 1: Understand that your mom or dad is insecure about losing you to your other parent and stepparent.

Step 2: Make sure your parent knows you have no intention of replacing him or her. For example, Yolanda could say to her mom, "I do have a good time at Dad's house, but Rosalie could never replace you because you're my mother, and I love you." This may seem simplistic, but sometimes parents need to be reassured, just as you do.

Step 3: Ask your parent whether he or she *wants* to hear the details of your visits. If he or she says no, you need to respect that. If your parent says yes, you can make a deal that you'll tell, but he or she can't act in a way that will make you uncomfortable. If that happens, you'll stop sharing the details. Then stick to it—you don't have to agree to be subjected to the "punishing" behavior because your parent doesn't like what you say.

Step 4: Remember, while you should be sensitive to your parent's feelings, you shouldn't feel guilty about enjoying yourself with your other family. Your parents are adults and will have to figure out how to manage their feelings.

What if it doesn't work . . . ?

We're not advocates of lying. But some parents really can't handle your relationship with your other family and also can't deal with not knowing what you do there (nagging you constantly for details even though they hate hearing it). And if you're suffering in the process, it may be easier for everyone if you simplify the story, keep it brief. For example: "We went to the movies in the afternoon and we spent the rest of the day hanging around."

Be clear in your own head why you're doing this
(because you're entitled to a guilt-free relationship
with your family), and don't allow it to spill over to
other situations.

**My dad discusses everything I tell him
with my stepmother. I can't trust him to
keep a secret anymore.**

> **Andrew:** I used to tell my dad everything.
> Then I found out he's sharing it all with his
> wife...even the *really* personal stuff! I'm
> mortified and he really let me down.

Ever since he could remember, Andrew's dad, Bill,
has been the person Andrew could trust with all his
private feelings. When he was young, they discussed
school, friends, and nightmares. When he was nine
or ten, they talked about sports, tests, and then, of
course, the divorce. As Andrew became older, they
talked about relationships, dreams, and the future.

He felt really lucky because, despite the divorce,

he and his dad had become closer than ever before. It was a hard adjustment for Andrew when Bill began dating again. It was weird seeing his dad with a woman other than his mother, and Andrew also felt that Lois, the girlfriend, was cutting into the time he and Bill shared. But they talked about it the way they talked about everything, and Bill assured Andrew that nothing would change between them. So when Bill and Lois married, Andrew was okay with it. But one day, Lois said she knew that Andrew was unhappy that he didn't have a girlfriend. She reassured Andrew that he shouldn't worry because he was good-looking, smart, and nice and would meet someone in time. She meant well, of course, but Andrew couldn't believe his dad had violated his trust by sharing something so private with Lois. He vowed that he would never again share anything private with his dad.

Andrew's story sparked quite a debate between Rachel and Marco, two of the other stepteens in Andrew's counseling group. Rachel felt Andrew's dad had proven himself unworthy and that Andrew was right never to trust him again. Marco said that although it was a major mistake, it is forgivable. The argument raged on for days so finally we decided that Rachel and Marco would have an official debate. Each would have one minute to present their side. We even invited other kids (not all stepteens) to participate so we could have a vote afterward. They drew straws and Rachel went first.

Rachel's Reasoning

For many years Andrew trusted his dad with important matters. Then Bill met Lois, and he decided his relationship with her was more important than his son's trust in him. It seems to me that Bill shared Andrew's secrets as a way to show Lois he wouldn't keep secrets from her. In my opinion, this demonstrates that Bill has given up his allegiance to Andrew for a relationship with Lois. This is why I feel Andrew can't trust Bill again. Bill wants his marriage to work and has sacrificed Andrew to make that happen.

Marco's Reasoning

There's no question that Bill has violated Andrew's trust. The question is whether it's forgivable. In my opinion, we have to look at Andrew's history with his dad to decide. Andrew had an excellent relationship with Bill until he married Lois. So we have to ask why Bill did what he did. Maybe Bill's problems in his first marriage made him insecure, so he needed to prove his love for Lois by sharing everything with her. Bill made a bad decision, but for an understandable reason. Andrew shouldn't give up on his dad. He doesn't know how lucky he is to have had such a close relationship with a parent. I'm sure if he tells Bill how bad he feels they'll be able to fix things.

Before you read the result of the group's voting, cast your own vote.

Now for the results . . . of the 27 voters, 19 voted
for Marco and 8 for Rachel. In a discussion after
the vote, the strongest feeling was that Andrew
should not risk losing a special relationship with his
dad without trying to repair it first. People make
mistakes but we should try to forgive and move
on, especially if the person is a valuable part of
our lives.

Don't assume that a parent's mistake, no matter
how big, means the end of your relationship. If
you've been close to your mom and dad all along,
tell your parent you're hurt and ask—no, demand—
that your parent stop telling your stepparent private
things. Understanding your parent's position in the
new marriage will help you to be forgiving.

What if it doesn't work . . . ?

It is unlikely that your parent will break a
confidence again after you explain how important it
is to you. However, if your parent refuses to stop
telling his or her spouse your secrets, you will
probably have to make the decision to stop

confiding in your parent. It really is a shame, but as in all the other situations we discuss, you can only be responsible for yourself. You will need to find another adult whom you can trust. Your other parent may work, or an aunt, uncle, or grandparent. In fact, a close friend's parent may be an excellent choice to share important issues with, or to get advice from.

Chapter Five
This Really Isn't Working For Me

Sometimes it feels like nothing is going right in your stepfamily. In fact, you may be thinking things will never be right again. But hang in there, because you will probably be able to manage even the toughest of stepliving problems.

My stepfather acts like I'm in the way and we argue all the time. But my mom doesn't even realize it's happening.

> **Miles:** My mom is so in love she's oblivious to how badly my stepfather treats me. In fact, he'd be happy if I moved in with my dad and left him alone with my mom.

We talked with Miles to understand what was going on with his mother and stepfather. Miles told us that he felt his stepfather disliked him from the very beginning and that he disliked his stepfather, as well. He has never discussed his feelings with his mom or stepfather because he thinks they don't really care.

"My mom is so in love," he said, "that she wouldn't even care if I moved out."

"Is it possible your mom doesn't realize how you feel and that your stepdad is having a hard time adjusting to the instant family?" we asked.

Miles felt hurt and was angered by our question. He felt we were taking sides and were trying to get his mom and stepdad off the hook. It was apparent that this was a sensitive subject to Miles and that there were "bad vibes" going both ways between him and his stepdad. Here is the feedback we offered to Miles.

You can't treat someone badly and still expect him or her to be nice to you. However, you do have a right to be upset. Many kids are upset when their mom or dad remarries. But if you refuse to give your stepparent a chance just because he or she isn't your favorite type of person, that makes the ignoring, yelling, and aggravation at least partially your fault. Your step is an adult, so he or she should be more understanding about your difficult adjustment. But your step also has feelings, and it must be hard to be rejected by a stepchild. **Stepparents can't be expected to maintain perfect behavior in the face of constant hostility.**

Kids need to take responsibility for telling their mom or dad how they feel. In Miles's case, he was convinced that he didn't matter to his mom, but he assumed this without giving her a chance. His mom probably *is* somewhat preoccupied with her new husband, which is understandable. If your parent is distracted, then it is really up to you to bring up the way you are feeling. You have to *tell your mom or dad how you feel.* It's the only way things will change. Keeping your feelings secret and walking around with a hostile attitude will not help you in any way!

What if it doesn't work . . . ?

Occasionally, you come across someone who doesn't adjust well to having stepkids and really treats them poorly. If this happens to you, and talking to your parent and stepparent doesn't work, you will have to take more serious action. If it's an option, consider spending more time, or even living, with your other parent. You can also spend more time with friends, with relatives, or in your room. Stay as far away from bad treatment as possible. Do not allow yourself to feel as if you are worthless because your parent or stepparent is neglecting you. That is their problem, and it is not a reflection on you. Before you back off a relationship with your parent and stepparent, make sure that you've taken an honest look at your own behavior. If your attitude is sending negative, alienating signals, try being more positive—you may get the same in return.

> My stepmother changed everything in my dad's house—from wallpaper to towels. It was fine the way it was, and she's ruined it.

> **Josie:** There's nothing left from how things used to be. It's not fair, and I hate it.

Josie and Kate, her stepmother, met with two teens (Carrie and Matt) who each lived in a stepfamily to discuss the friction between them. Kate explained that when she married Josie's dad she really wanted to move to a new house and start fresh, but they couldn't afford to move. Instead, they decided they would redo Josie's dad's house. Kate emphasized that she really didn't want to live in a house that someone else had decorated. "Actually," she said, "I thought it was very pretty and nicely decorated, but it wasn't mine. I know Josie is insulted and upset but she needs to understand that this has nothing to do with her, or my feelings for her. I just want my marriage and home to belong to me, without the memory of someone who was here before me. I'm sorry Josie is angry with me, but there's nothing I can do about that."

Josie said that she was very upset with the changes. "I cry myself to sleep every night because there's nothing left of my old life," she said. "I wish I still had my mom and dad together and that nothing had changed. But at least I had the house to remind me of how our life used to be. Now there's nothing." She added that she actually liked Kate's taste but it seemed disrespectful to her mom that Kate and her dad changed everything.

Matt told Josie and Kate that he thought the problem was that Kate never told Josie why she wanted to redo the house. He felt it was understandable that Kate didn't want to live in the shadow of Josie's mother but that should've been talked out. Carrie agreed. And so did Kate and Josie. Here are some suggestions derived from our discussion:

Suggestions for Stepkids

1. Show this chapter to your parents
and stepparents.

2. Tell them how you feel about the changes,
especially if you feel sad.

3. Ask to be included in the decision-making so you
don't feel left out.

4. Ask your stepparent to explain why he or she
wants to change things. Do not view change
as disrespecting you or your other parent.

Suggestions for Stepparents

1. Discuss your feelings with your spouse about
living in a house that someone else decorated.

2. Include your stepkids in any changes you plan to
make to the house.

3. Allow your stepkids to keep their own bedrooms
unchanged.

4. Ask your stepkids if there are any special items
from the "old house" that they would like to
keep in their room or pack away to use in their
own home as adults.

5. If you move to a new home, include your stepkids as much as possible in the search for and decoration of the new place.

What if it doesn't work . . . ?

Life doesn't always work the way you want, so it's possible that your parents will do what they want despite how you feel. You will need to dig down deep and find some understanding that new stepparents usually feel threatened by moving into territory that is not theirs. Your support (despite how you feel) will go a long way to making your stepparent feel more comfortable in his or her new home, and then your stepparent probably will be more receptive to your feelings. Look at the positives—change can be a good thing!

My mom and I used to spend lots of time together. Now we always have to include my stepdad and his kids. I really miss our private time.

> **Patty:** I bet regular families don't spend every minute together the way my stepfamily does. Can't I ever be alone with my mom anymore?

This is a good time to look at the differences between step and "regular" families because it may help to explain why things have changed.

☞ In regular families, the adults learned to be parents by sharing a baby and watching that child grow up. In stepfamilies, adults have to learn to parent someone else's child who has already done a lot of growing up before they even appeared on the scene.

☞ Regular families have been together since the children were babies. They are used to being together and don't have to spend all of their time together. Stepfamilies have to practice being together because it's new for them, which means they need to spend *lots* of time together.

☞ Parents in regular families can easily spend time alone with one child because everyone's relationships are secure. In stepfamilies, kids may feel their stepparent doesn't love them if they are left out, so parents and stepparents are more likely to include the whole family in activities.

Patty's mom may be spending less time alone with Patty because she doesn't want Patty's stepsiblings to feel left out. It doesn't mean Patty and her mom shouldn't work out some private time together *without* anyone getting hurt. Here are some suggestions:

☞ Plan a regular time each week when you do something alone with your parent (dinner, a tennis game, library time, a movie, or any other activity you enjoy together).

☞ Ask your parent to make sure your stepsibs have other plans (with a parent, friend, grandparent, etc.) so they don't feel left out, and your parent doesn't feel guilty.

☞ Plan ten or fifteen minutes every day alone with your parent, just to catch up on the day and feelings or thoughts you haven't had time to share with each other.

What if it doesn't work . . . ?

There are a couple of reasons it may be difficult for you to get time alone with your mom or dad. If the stepfamily is only a few months old, it may be too soon. Realistically, your parent has to juggle a lot, helping everyone get used to being a family. Maybe wait a little longer before having this chat. If the family isn't new, and you've tried talking to your parent without success, you will need to find another way to get your parent's attention. Try a letter or e-mail expressing your concerns. Take the time to express yourself clearly. Consider including some of the following thoughts: I miss you. I understand that you are juggling a lot but is there a way to set aside time for you and me?

You had a close relationship once, and with some effort, you can have it again.

My stepmother tries so hard to be nice that it gets on my nerves. How can I tell her without hurting her feelings?

Alec: My stepmom gets on my nerves twenty-four seven. She really wants me to like her and always tries to make me happy. But I feel stifled and don't know how to tell her.

All the stepteens we spoke to agreed that this is

a sticky subject. Obviously, it's better to have a stepparent who *wants* a relationship with you than one who doesn't. But if a stepparent doesn't give the relationship a chance to develop naturally, it won't work, either. The teens also felt it would be really difficult to talk to a stepparent about this face-to-face. Based on this feedback, we've come up with a model of a letter you can give, send, or e-mail to your stepparent to help you get your point across in a sensitive yet meaningful way.

Dear _____ (fill in your stepparent's name),
I've noticed that you've been trying really hard to get to know me and spend time with me. I have seen lots of stepparents who don't make an effort with their stepkids, so I really appreciate what you're doing. I just want to mention that sometimes it feels like you try too hard to make our relationship work. I understand that you really want us to get along, and I want that, too. I think that I just need a bit more time to feel comfortable with

our relationship. You don't have to try extra hard to be nice, or to do everything, or to spend all your time with me. I definitely want to spend time with you and get to know you better. I think it may just take me a bit longer than you thought it would take. If you want to write back or talk to me about this letter, that would be great.

Thanks for listening,

_____(your name)

What if it doesn't work . . . ?

It's still much better to have a stepparent who really likes you and wants to have a relationship than one who doesn't. So try to appreciate that fact. And remember, the more effort you make with your stepparent, the less they'll feel they have to work to relate to you. Things will become more relaxed and less aggravating for you.

My dad married his affair, and they expect me to be happy for them. I hate her, and I'm furious with him. So get real, Dad!

> *Stacey:* I'll never forgive my dad for having an affair and ruining everything. I don't know how he can expect me to have anything to do with his new wife. I don't want to visit them or even talk to them.

There's no question that when your mom or dad has an affair, it affects how much you trust him or her. You may feel like your parent betrayed the whole family and even caused the divorce. As angry as you may be, try to remember that everyone makes mistakes. And although this is a huge one, the question is whether it's something you should forgive. A group of teens came up with this quiz to help you decide whether you're making the right decision by boycotting your parent and his or her new spouse.

Forgive Them or Forget Them?

Answer True or False to each question.

1. I hate the new spouse enough to risk   (T)   F
ruining my relationship with my parent
by rejecting my new stepparent.

2. I *really* feel things will get better if I   T   (F)
remain angry with my parent and my
new stepparent.

3. My parent makes no effort to help   (T)   F
me overcome feeling betrayed.

4. My parent and I weren't close long   T   (F)
before the affair.

5. I want to get over feeling betrayed   (T)   F
and feel better about my stepparent.

6. I had a good relationship with   (T)   F
my parent before the affair.

7. The new spouse really isn't a bad person,   T   ⓕ
except for ruining my parents' marriage.

8. There are other people (friends, family, etc.) T   ⓕ
encouraging me to hate my parent and
the "affair."

So, how did you score? If you answered *True* to the first four statements and *False* to the last four, it's a good bet that your relationship with your parent was tense, angry, or sad long before the divorce. The affair just made it worse. You will need help to work things out. This is a good time to find someone you trust who can give you the support you need to repair your relationship with your parent. If it seems the relationship is beyond repair now, you may need to look elsewhere for the parenting relationship you're missing. Perhaps a counselor, a teacher, or a close relative can be helpful. But don't close any doors. Relationships can change, and parents and children can come to terms with each other as they settle into new lives.

If you answered *False* to any of the first four questions, or *True* to any of the last four, you may want to think twice about whether you're ready to write off your relationship with your parent (and the new spouse). Your parent made a big mistake, which may even feel like betrayal, but the truth is you don't *really* know what happened between your parents. You don't know what events led up to the affair. In all likelihood, their marriage wasn't great and would have ended in divorce anyway. So if you're honest with yourself, you'll admit that the affair, and the new spouse, probably didn't cause the divorce, but rather was the result of a marriage already in trouble.

That brings us to your relationship with your parent and your new stepparent. If you and your parent had a good relationship before the affair and you wish you still did, you should be able to repair it now—particularly if your parent is already making an effort to do so. Open yourself up to the possibility that in time you could like your stepparent, despite the circumstances. If another person (especially your other parent, who probably still feels very betrayed) tries to convince you otherwise, ask that parent not to discuss it with you (see chapter 4). It may take time and certainly effort by everyone, but in the long run it will be worth the hard work. Your parent loves you, and despite the mistakes that have been made, it's likely you still love them. Forgiveness will be worth it.

What if it doesn't work . . . ?

If you can't overcome feeling betrayed even though you want to, you should probably think about getting some counseling. A good place to start is a guidance counselor, school psychologist, or school social worker. They have lots of experience helping kids with all sorts of problems. If they can't help you, they will be able to help find someone who can. It's really important not to keep serious feelings like betrayal locked up inside you. You'd be surprised how talking to someone can help, especially someone who is trained in this area.

My dad left the family because there was so much fighting. So why can't I leave this stepfamily for the same reason?

> *Luke:* My mom and stepdad are fighting all the time so I want to move in with my dad.

1. Do you *really* want to move out? Is this an impulsive decision or is it something you've been thinking about for a long time? Don't decide that you want to move out when you're angry or during a fight. You may regret it later. Rather, during a calm time, let your parent know how unhappy you are. Ask your parent to make some changes. And then try to remember that your real parents' divorce was not decided casually. No one moved out because of a little fighting. It wasn't *all* one person's fault. It was a big decision that occurred after a great deal of thought and serious problems. But if you are really miserable, and the situation is affecting your life dramatically, moving out may be worth considering.

2. Do you have somewhere to go? Would your other parent, grandparents, or an aunt or uncle take you in, and is theirs a home that would be appropriate for a teenager? For example, your single, twenty-four-year-old aunt who is out every night until midnight is *not* a good option. Would you be willing to move away from siblings, switch schools, or even move to a different area if necessary? Would the new situation actually be better than the one you're in now? For example, if your alternative is your grandparents with whom you have never seen eye-to-eye, you may want to reconsider.

3. Are you willing to fight to convince your parent it's what you want? There is a good chance you'll have to argue for weeks or even months to move out. If you can't stand up to your parent, you're less likely to succeed. Are you willing to risk alienating yourself from your parent through this process? Most parents will not take this request lightly. They will be extremely hurt and angry.

4. Are you prepared to undergo a legal battle if necessary? Depending on where you live and your age, you, and the person agreeing to take you, may have to go to court to facilitate your move. You may have to testify in court (or privately to a judge) about your unhappiness in your stepfamily. This would probably mean saying negative things about your parent, which could make you feel bad and your parent feel even more angry and more hurt. You would have to be prepared to do this because a judge may not allow you to move without a legitimate reason.

If you are able to work out all of the above issues, give one final thought to whether moving out is what you really want. Try not to close any doors when you move. In other words, ask your parent to consider allowing you to move back if things don't work out. But don't be surprised if your parent responds negatively at first. Your parent may feel so rejected by you that he or she will refuse to allow you to come back. You have to be prepared for this possibility.

On the other hand, your parent may try to improve things after you move out and then invite you back home. Of course, this would be the best outcome, but don't count on it. Chronic fighting in more than one marriage may be a sign that your parent hasn't figured out how to have a good relationship, and may never do so.

What if it doesn't work . . . ?

If you're stuck in a really bad situation with no options for getting out, you will have to take care of yourself. Recognize that you don't have to fight, curse, yell, or criticize just because members of your family and stepfamily choose these ways to communicate. You have complete control over your actions, even if you can't control those around you. You are old enough to make choices that are more socially acceptable. Speak politely and calmly to others, and don't fight just because things aren't going your way. Find healthier role models in your friends, their families, teachers, and your extended family members. Eventually you'll move out, and these skills will help you for the rest of your life.

Chapter Six
Sorting out Confusing Feelings

There are so many conflicting feelings when you're in a stepfamily that you may not be able to predict what you'll be feeling from day to day. Sometimes things will seem great, but other times you may wish it could all go back to the way it was before the stepfamily.

Sometimes I wish my father and stepmother would divorce, and my parents would get back together. The truth is that everyone is happy the way things are now, so why do I feel this way?

Jessica: My parents have been divorced for four years and they're both remarried, but I *still* think about them getting back together. What is wrong with me?

There is nothing wrong with Jessica, you, or any kid who sometimes wishes his or her parents could be back together, even if the parents are happily remarried! As you may know from experience, divorce means your family is breaking apart forever. The sadness you feel about that may never go away.

Larry, a twenty-six-year-old, told us: "My parents divorced when I was twelve, and I still sometimes wish they were together." And if one of your parents has died, that sad feeling might be even worse. You wish your mom or dad was still alive and your life could go back to the way it was. Julia's dad died in a car crash when she was three and now, at fifteen, Julia still fantasizes about what her life would be like if she had both her parents. It may seem strange to you, but in some ways death and divorce often feel similar for kids. In both situations, you will never be able to get back the life you used to have, no matter how much you wish for it.

After divorcing, your parents were probably alone for a while before they started to feel like sharing their lives with other adults again. Then they started dating other people and eventually decided to remarry. Of course, you probably had all kinds of feelings when your parents began dating. You may have felt that if either one remarried, it would be even harder for them to get back together. You may have been angry because remarriage forced you to admit that your parents would never reunite. But now, here they are remarried, and you're *still* thinking about them together. As you can see, the wish to have your parents together is very powerful *no matter what the reality of your life*. It does not mean you're crazy, weird, or any of the other things you may worry about. It's perfectly normal to want your parents together, and just about every child of divorce feels that way for some period of his or her life.

Knowing your feelings are normal may not be enough to make you feel better. So we asked some teens and young adults how they've helped themselves manage these sad and confusing longings.

✖ I list the pros and cons of my parents' remarrying. It reminds me how much they used to fight and I stop wishing they would get back together.

✖ I tell myself there are some things I couldn't control, like my mom dying, but at least my dad remarried and I have a really nice stepmother.

✖ I write about my feelings in a special diary.

✖ I allow myself an hour a week to think about my parents being together. I imagine it as much as possible during that time. It's enough so that the rest of the time I can focus on reality.

✖ I write poetry as a way to express my feelings. One poem was even published in the school paper.

✖ I realize my mom is much happier now than when my parents argued all the time. That makes it easier to be happy myself.

✖ I remind myself that there are kids who have much worse problems than I do.

✖ I talk to my stepsister a lot because she understands my feelings since she feels the same way.

✖ I promise myself I will do things differently when I'm an adult. I will be careful when I marry, so I don't get divorced, and my kids won't have to be sad.

✖ I think about how much I love my baby brother, and I know I wouldn't have him if my dad hadn't remarried.

As you can see, the way you *think* about your life can have a *huge* impact on the way you *feel*. Have you heard the saying "If life gives you lemons, make lemonade"? It means you can find something sweet even in a sour situation. You can try doing that, too. You have much more control than you may realize, and you can refocus yourself to look at the positives instead of just the negatives.

What if it doesn't work . . . ?

Are thoughts about your parents being together preoccupying you? Maybe you can't concentrate on schoolwork, friends, or other activities. You feel depressed, have trouble sleeping (or sleep too much), have no interest in food (or eat too much), or feel like crying all the time. If this description fits, you should tell your mom, dad, a school counselor, or even the school nurse. There is no reason for you to feel this way, and these people can help you, so don't keep it to yourself.

I always compare my real parent to my stepparent. I don't know how to stop myself.

Carlos: I feel guilty because I wish my father were more like my stepfather.

Annie: My stepmother isn't as sweet or warm as my mom, and I compare them all the time.

If you think about it, life is all about comparisons. Do you like this shirt or that one? This snack or that one? Do you like one friend better than another? One teacher? One baby-sitting job? One coach? It's impossible not to compare, and this goes for parents as well. In fact, if you have two moms or two dads (one step and one regular) it seems almost impossible not to compare. There are always things you'll like better about one parent than another because everyone has their strengths and weaknesses. While comparisons are hard to avoid, they might make you focus on a parent or stepparent's flaws. That can only cause stress in your relationships. Check out Carlos's and Annie's stories and you'll see what we mean.

Carlos has a terrific relationship with Alex, his stepdad. Alex participates in all Carlos's sports and activities and always helps with his homework. On the other hand, Carlos's real father doesn't make much effort to be involved in Carlos's life. In fact, lately, Carlos has been wishing Alex was his father. And he's also angry that his real dad isn't more like Alex.

Annie gets along well with her stepmother, Amy. They spend time together playing tennis and shopping, and Amy is really interested in her life. But Annie can't help comparing Amy to her real mother, who died three years ago. She remembers that her mom used to hug her a lot and tell her she loved her. Secretly, Annie wishes Amy was more like her mom used to be, but Amy doesn't show her feelings in that way. Yet at the same time, Annie feels terrible for comparing because she really thinks Amy is a wonderful stepmother.

Annie and Carlos need some ways to manage their feelings so they can enjoy their relationships with all of their parents. Kyle's mom remarried twice, so he was a stepteen twice over. He is twenty-seven now and has certainly had many opportunities to compare parents. He has created some techniques for managing these complicated feelings and agreed to share them with all of us.

Controlling the Comparisons

☞ Realize that it's impossible *not* to compare.

☞ If a parent or stepparent really is a better parent, admit it to yourself without feeling guilty. You haven't done anything wrong by acknowledging the truth.

☞ Accept the limitations of all of your parents and stepparents. One of your parents may have died and can no longer be part of your life. Or maybe your parent is just not a very good parent and doesn't make much of an effort to see you.

☞ Get whatever you can out of each relationship. Some relationships will give you a lot, and some just a little. Some parents may not be able to give you emotional support, but may give you financial support, and vice versa. Over time, things may change. For example, a parent who can't give you much now may turn out to be a better parent later on.

☞ As much as possible, look at each parent and stepparent as an individual. The reason someone is good or bad at parenting has a lot to do with how that person was treated as a child.

☞ Don't verbalize your comparisons to your parents and stepparents. The negative ones will hurt and even the "positive" ones may hurt someone else. (If a parent told you that you were much better at something than your brother, it might make you feel good for a second, but then you would wonder why they were putting down your brother by complimenting you. It's the same if you compare your parents to each other.)

☞ If you do need to get something off your chest, share any disappointment or frustration with other people you trust.

What if it doesn't work . . . ?

If your parent and stepparent are so different that you just can't help comparing them all the time, it's probably because there is a drastic difference in how they each parent you. Focus on your relationship with the one who is parenting you in a healthier, more beneficial way. You may also want to speak to someone about feeling sad or angry if a parent or stepparent has really disappointed you.

When my dad and stepmom argue, I am afraid they will also get divorced.

> *Tyrone:* I was sure my dad and stepmom would be together forever, until I heard them yelling at each other. Now I worry they'll divorce like my mom and dad did.

If you're like Tyrone, and get butterflies in your stomach every time your parent and stepparent fight, you're not alone. In fact, you may be surprised to know that most kids, whether they live with both parents or with a parent and a stepparent, worry when they hear fighting. We hear about and see so much divorce around us, even on our favorite TV shows, that it's hard not to think about it. And for the teens who have been through divorce, it's even more understandable that the yelling causes worry. Tyrone told us his parents fought for years before they finally divorced. In the beginning, they reassured him their fighting did not mean they would divorce. So now Tyrone is skeptical when his dad and stepmom (Ron and Vivienne) reassure him that their fighting doesn't imply the end of their marriage. "I want to believe them," explained Tyrone, "but I panic when I sense a fight coming. In fact, I do everything I can to stop them from arguing. You know I'd give *anything* to keep them together." Even though he admits they argue only once in a while, Tyrone is *really* stressing.

Ron and Vivienne are both concerned about Tyrone and want him to feel better. But they also feel strongly that their occasional disagreements are nothing like the fights Tyrone's parents had before divorcing. They feel bad for Tyrone and have tried to reassure him. But they also don't want to live forever in the shadow of his parents' marriage. We agree that as long as the marriage is good, Tyrone will have to learn to respond differently to the arguing at home. We suggested that to make this easier for him, they try hard not to fight in front of Tyrone. If a teen doesn't have to hear a parent and stepparent fight, it gives him or her time to become secure about the marriage without worrying about what happened to his or her parents' marriage.

We spoke to Tyrone, as well, and these are the suggestions we gave him:

☞ **Ask your parents/stepparents not to fight in front of you.** Explain that it is harder for you to trust that their marriage will last if you hear them fighting.

☞ **If you happen to catch an argument, don't listen.** Leave the house, put on earphones, turn up the TV, or close your door.

☞ **Remember that everyone argues sometimes.** It's almost impossible for people to have close relationships without disagreeing or fighting once in a while. Don't you argue with your friends occasionally?

☞ **Voice your concerns.** When your parent and stepparent reassure you that their marriage is strong, use this as an opportunity to tell them why you are worried. They will probably be able to address most of your worries.

☞ **Recognize that you have been "burned."** The long-time fighting that occurred between your real parents had an effect on you. Admit to yourself that those feelings probably make you overly worried about other relationships. Look at your parent and stepparent's marriage as a completely different relationship. If you can do this you won't feel so worried.

☞ **Remember it is not your responsibility to end the arguing**. Adults need to work out differences themselves. However, you can certainly remind them not to fight in front of you.

What if it doesn't work . . . ?

If your parent and stepparent argue a lot, and if their fights are really serious, you may have reason to worry. However, you will need to accept that there is nothing you can do about it. Don't get involved because it will just make you feel worse.

You may have to deal with the possibility that this marriage won't make it. Keeping this in mind will make it easier for you to accept if it does end. If the fighting is not bad, but you just can't shake the anxiety and worry, you might consider suggesting to your parents that your family attend therapy together. A family therapist would meet with all of you and help you work out the things that worry you. They could even give your parents some suggestions for how to handle their disputes differently. Lots of teens ask for help in this way and it is nothing that should make you feel weird or embarrassed.

My mom always closes the door when she and my stepdad are alone in their room. She used to leave it open all the time, so now I feel shut out. Why do they need so much privacy?

Becky: They must be having sex, why else would they need to keep their door closed all the time?

Privacy is an interesting thing. We love to get it, but it's hard to give it. Take this quiz and see how many privacy points you score.

Getting Privacy Quiz

1. Do you have your own bedroom?   Y **N**

2. Do you have your own bathroom?   Y **N**

3. Can you listen to your music when you   **Y** **N**
want to without having to fight for
the stereo?

4. Are there house rules preventing others   Y **N**
from barging into your room when they want?

5. Do you have somewhere to keep private   **Y** N
things (diary, letters, etc.)?

6. Can you talk on the phone privately?   Y **N**

7. Do you have somewhere private to hang   **Y** N
out with your friends?

8. Is there a family understanding preventing   Y **N**
sibs and stepsibs from always tagging along
with you?

9. Do your parents accept that you won't   **Y** N
share every minute of your life with them?

10. If you leave your belongings, food, or **Y** **N**
clothes in a communal area of the house, do
you feel they will be left alone?

Scoring: *Give yourself one point for each yes and zero
points for each no.*

Privacy is Protected (7-10 points): Your privacy is
appreciated and respected in your house. Everyone
realizes that you need time to be by yourself or
alone with another person. You may not have a
perfect scenario (your own bedroom or bathroom),
but the message is clear. Everyone should be able to
have privacy when he or she needs it. But
remember, this includes your parents. You may not
have thought about it as much before the
remarriage (privacy may not be such a big issue for
a single parent). But now that your parent is married
again, you might feel weird because your parent and
stepparent don't leave the doors open anymore. But
adults need privacy for many different reasons—
talking, arguing, and even . . . dare we say it . . . sex!

It doesn't mean they are "doing it" every time the door is closed. When people are in a new relationship they need time alone, just to be together. This may make other people in the family feel a bit left out, but try to remember how much you enjoy *your* privacy.

Privacy isn't Perfect (4-6 points): It's probably a bit tough for you, or anyone else in your home, to find time alone. There may not be enough space, and there probably aren't enough rules protecting people's rights to privacy. It's understandable that you may be a bit resentful that your parents can just close their door when they want to be alone. The truth is, sometimes it's easier for adults to get privacy than it is for kids. Adults can demand it, or they can close or lock their bedroom door. If you had more privacy yourself, you would probably be more understanding of your parents' need for it, as well. Perhaps you can talk to them about enforcing some rules that protect your stuff and give you time alone, or with friends, in your room. But remember, *you* will have to respect your parents' right to privacy *and* the right to privacy of other kids in the family.

Privacy is a Problem (0-3): It's no surprise you're hurt and angry that your parent and stepparent want time alone because privacy is generally unheard of in your family. In homes where little or no importance is placed on the need for privacy, it can be very difficult for kids to get used to the idea that a new marriage means their dad or mom now wants time alone. If you have grown up in this kind of home, you probably experience the closed door as a real rejection. It's not really your fault that you feel this way because it's what you've been accustomed to your whole life. Nevertheless, you are going to have to get used to the fact that a new relationship means your parent and stepparent will want privacy sometimes. It doesn't mean that they don't love you and it doesn't mean that they're trying to exclude you from their lives. Take this opportunity to discuss your need for privacy and ask your parents to help you find ways to get time alone.

What if it doesn't work . . . ?

Do your parent and stepparent spend *all* their time behind closed doors? Perhaps they are so caught up in their new marriage that they don't even realize they're shutting out the rest of the world. But since they have kids to take care of, this is not really acceptable. You (and your stepsibs, if you have any) will have to talk to them about how they are behaving. Tell them that, although you understand they need time alone, you also need their attention and feel very much left out. If this doesn't work, ask a close adult friend or relative to speak to them for you.

My parents say they will always love me, even though they are remarried, but how can I be sure? After all, they used to love each other, right?

Patrick: I can't help wondering if my parents will stop loving me if I do something bad, like getting an F at school or having a huge fight with them.

It's not unusual for teens to worry that, since their parents stopped loving each other, they could stop loving them, too. (This is especially true for kids who have been adopted because they often feel one set of parents has already given them up.) But if this were true, it would mean that the love of a parent for a child is the same as the love of one adult for another. In reality, parental love is very different from the love between a couple. (Are your feelings for your boyfriend or girlfriend the same as your feelings for your parents?) We asked a group of teens to describe how the two emotions are different. Their perceptions will help you understand why your parents won't stop loving you, even if they stopped loving each other.

✖ A couple falls in love because they have many things in common and they get along with each other. Parents love their children because they choose to have or adopt them, before they even know what their personality, likes, or dislikes will be like.

✖ A couple stays in love because they continue working to improve their relationship. A parent's love for a child doesn't depend on work (although a really close relationship may require work by everyone).

✖ A couple has to have an equal and mutually respectful relationship to work well. But a parent-child relationship is usually *not* equal (the parent is in charge)—although hopefully there is mutual respect.

✖ A couple gets divorced because their relationship doesn't work anymore. Here are some reasons for a couple's relationship to stop working:

1. Never agreeing on anything.
2. Big fights all the time.
3. One or both having an affair.
4. Different philosophies about life (religion, raising children, working).
5. Money problems.
6. Married when they were young and then drift apart or falling out of love.
7. Constantly bickering.
8. Never happy together.
9. One or both abusing drugs or alcohol.
10. Physical or emotional abuse by one to the other.

Even though problems can arise between parents and children also, parents love their children through thick and thin. Parents understand that kids (even teens) are still learning about life. They love their children and want to help them learn. Their love isn't contingent on good grades or good behavior. In fact, parents' love for their children is almost always unconditional. They love their children no matter what and would never even consider any other alternative. That's not to say they'll always approve of your grades and behavior, but being upset, angry, or disappointed isn't the same as not loving you anymore. The standards and expectations for loving a partner and loving a child are simply not the same.

What if it doesn't work . . . ?

Occasionally, kids feel their parents' love really is contingent on things like grades and behavior. And generally, this has nothing to do with being divorced or remarried. Some parents are so caught up in those things that they think their children will do better or try harder if the parents withhold loving feelings. This doesn't feel very good to the kid (as you know if you've experienced it), and it's something your mom or dad may need a lot of help to realize. It's unlikely that you'll be able to do it alone, so you should speak to a close adult or counselor to get some help. You can and should tell yourself that just because your parent doesn't always act lovingly, doesn't mean you're not lovable. Look for other adults who can help you to feel better about yourself.

My stepfather wants to adopt me, and I'm not sure how I feel about it.

> **Maya:** I'm fourteen, and my dad died when I was three. My mom and I have been living with my stepdad since I was five. He asked if he could adopt me. I love him, but I just can't decide.

Being adopted is a major event for you and your stepparent. He or she now wants to legally be your parent. This means being responsible for your welfare, education, and future, equally with your real parent. It also means that if something bad happened to your parent, your stepparent would assume complete responsibility for you and continue to take care of you. Adopting a stepchild is a statement of love and commitment, and it's generally a decision that is not made lightly.

But what about you, the stepchild—how do you feel about being adopted? For some kids, it's a simple decision. If you've been with your stepparent a long time, have a close relationship, and if you don't really remember your mom or dad, you will probably feel that it's natural and positive. You probably already consider your stepparent to be your mother or father, so being adopted won't really change your life. But it's not always that simple. Some kids are ambivalent about being adopted, especially when they're in their teens.

Here are the things teens have told us can make them unsure:

1. Feeling guilty that you're betraying your parent by replacing him or her with your adoptive parent.

2. Feeling you'll give up some of your history.

3. Feeling sad because it means your other parent *really* won't come back (even though you probably knew it anyway).

4. Being unsure of what it will mean in the future.

5. Worrying that you'll let yourself get too close, and then your step/adoptive parent will leave you, too.

6. Not liking your stepparent.

On the other hand, another group of teens suggested reasons why being adopted could be a really positive experience for you.

1. Having a strong, legal bond with someone you love and think of as a parent anyway.

2. Knowing that you have another adult who legally is responsible for your welfare and future should anything happen to your parent.

3. Knowing that your stepparent really loves you and is showing it in a big way.

4. Having the same last name as other people in your family.

5. Having a bigger extended family (grandparents, aunts, uncles, etc).

6. Not feeling conflicted when you call your stepparent Mom or Dad.

If you look at the two lists carefully, you will realize it's possible to have feelings from both, at the same time. For example, you may feel guilty that you're replacing your parent, but at the same time you may be excited and happy that your stepparent wants to adopt you. So being ambivalent doesn't mean that you shouldn't consider adoption.

To understand it better, let's go through the issues on the first list to see why they aren't good reasons to rule out adoption.

1. It is not unusual for teens to feel that being adopted means betraying a parent (especially when a parent has died). But all parents wish the best for their children, and having a loving, caring adoptive parent is exactly what your parent would have wished for you. Don't give up this opportunity for a valuable relationship because you feel guilty. Rather, talk about your feelings with your parent and stepparent. Once you air them, you will start to feel better. If your parent is not dead but has abandoned you in some way, you certainly should not feel guilt for allowing yourself to have a healthy parenting relationship with another person.

2. Being adopted doesn't erase your past life. You will always have memories, pictures, and stories. In fact, being adopted can enrich your life and give you an even fuller history.

3. Some kids hold a secret hope that one day their parent will return and want them back. However, it's important not to allow a fantasy or false hope to interfere with the reality of your current life. If you are close to your stepparent, give yourself a chance to move on, especially in cases where a parent has deserted the family.

4. The best way to find out what the future could bring is to speak openly to your parent and stepparent. Not knowing is not a reason to resist adoption. You will probably find that your stepparent's plans for the future include helping you to achieve your goals and enjoying watching you grow up.

5. Fear of loss is another common worry among teens who have experienced the death of a parent or abandonment by a parent. By refusing to be adopted, you think you can maintain a distance, and possibly keep yourself protected from another painful experience. But the truth is that it is highly unlikely that your stepparent will die an untimely death. And although there are never guarantees in life, if your stepparent is making the effort to adopt you, it is not likely that he or she will abandon you. Instead of denying yourself the chance to have a parent's support and love, talk about your fears of abandonment and loss. It may help to speak to a counselor who can help you understand and manage these feelings.

What if it doesn't work . . . ?

Now let's look at #6 on the first list. What if you *really* don't like your stepparent and don't want to be adopted by him or her? As a teenager, you probably don't have to be adopted against your will. Tell your mom or dad how you feel, and be clear that it is not something you want—at all. If your parent and stepparent insist on going through with it, be prepared to tell a judge how you feel. Most judges will listen seriously to the feelings of a teenager whose life will be changed dramatically.

Chapter Seven
Money Is a Huge Issue

How much money there is, and who gets it, can cause a lot of stress in a stepfamily. We all know how hard it can be when we feel we're being treated unfairly. This goes double for money issues.

My mom complains that my dad doesn't give her enough child support but he seems to spend a lot on his new wife.

Mara: Last weekend my stepmother was wearing an expensive sweater that my dad bought her. So why doesn't my mother get more money for us?

There are several issues that need to be addressed in this question. Child support can be a very confusing issue. To help you understand it a little better, we've outlined the issues the way you outline an essay.

Child Support: How Does It Work?

I. How do they figure out child support in the first place?

A. Who gives the money?

B. Who gets the money?

C. How much is it?

II. Does child support ever change?

A. Can it change if a parent's financial situation changes?

B. Can it change if a parent remarries?

III. What should I do if a parent complains about child support?

A. My mom is complaining we don't get enough money

B. My dad is complaining he has to give too much money

C. My stepparent is complaining.

IV. How should I get involved?

Now, let's fill in the details.

When two people with children get divorced, they figure out if one or both of them will take care of the children, and if one or both of them will pay money to support the children. This money is called *child support.*

The decision about which parent pays depends upon who works outside the home and who earns more money. If only one parent works, that person will have to contribute all the child support money. But if both parents work, they will both have to contribute. The amount each contributes will depend upon how much each makes.

The parent with whom the children live gets the money. If parents split the care, the money will be split.

An accountant works out how much money it takes to support the children. The exact amount depends upon how much money the parents earn. Sometimes, if the parents argue about it, a judge will tell each of them how much they must contribute.

Children often wonder if the amount of child

support ever changes. If a parent's financial situation changes, it is possible for child support to change, as well. For example, if your parent loses a job he or she may no longer be able to contribute the same amount, and a judge may allow him or her to pay less for a while. On the other hand, if the same parent starts making more money, he or she may have to increase the amount contributed.

What happens if a parent remarries? Remarriage by either parent does not have an effect on child support. No matter what your parents' life choices, they still have to take care of your financial needs. For example, even if your mom marries a super-rich guy, and your dad doesn't make much money, your dad *still* has to pay the same child support because you are his child and he has an *obligation* to support you. This is independent of anything your stepfather chooses to spend on you.

Sometimes parents complain about the amount of child support they give or receive. This is unfortunate because the kids usually get stuck in the middle of the fighting or feel guilty because, in a way, the fighting is about them. There's nothing you can do to stop the complaining. But you can probably stop them from complaining to you, and you certainly don't have to accept their complaints at face value.

Here's some advice about how to stay out of child support fights between parents. If your mom complains that she doesn't get enough child support because your dad spends it all on his new wife, you need to realize that neither you nor your mom knows what finances your dad's wife brought to the marriage. For example, maybe Mara's stepmother has lots of her own money, which she contributed to the marriage. This could be the reason for the expensive sweater. Mara's stepmother has no obligation to support Mara. Even if Mara's dad's lifestyle has improved through this new marriage, this money does not have to go to Mara's support. It may be infuriating to your mother to see her "replacement" getting more stuff than she or her kids get, but without knowing where the money comes from, complaining is unfair. *But*, even if one parent has a legitimate complaint because the other *really* doesn't contribute enough child support, it is absolutely inappropriate for your parent to complain to you. Check out chapter 4, and do not allow it to continue. Money issues should be kept private, between the adults.

Sometimes one parent complains about paying too much child support. Don't just accept this at face value. Unfortunately, some parents complain about child support no matter how much, or little, they have to pay. Others complain because they are bitter about the divorce or because the other parent has remarried. Of course, maybe your parent really is overpaying. For example, maybe your mom lost her job but the judge won't lower her child support payments. Nevertheless, the bottom line is the same: *It's unfair and wrong for your parent to talk to you about the financial stresses of child support.* It's hard enough being a kid of divorce and remarriage. You shouldn't have to be subjected to your parents' financial concerns, too.

Sometimes stepparents complain as well. A

stepmother may complain that her husband has to give so much money to his ex-wife and his kids that there isn't enough left for the two of them. This may or may not be true but since you don't know the financial details, you're not in a position to judge. If you're upset that she's complaining to *you*, you're right to feel this way. It's no different from a real parent voicing money complaints. Tell your parent and stepparent it makes you uncomfortable and walk away when you hear the conversation beginning.

It is also very important not to automatically believe one parent over the other. Take Mara, for example. She assumed her stepmother's expensive sweater meant her mom should get more child support. Mara's mother is resentful and angry and may feel she's owed more, even if it's not true. If your mother or father or a stepparent complains to you about money, try your hardest to resist automatically believing the complaints. Accepting the gripes as truth is guaranteed to have a negative affect on your relationship with your other parent, and who needs that?

What if it doesn't work . . . ?

If your parent really does avoid contributing to your support, you have a right to be very angry and hurt. It's a serious problem that could result in criminal charges against the offending parent. But it's still an adult issue, over which you have no control.

Ultimately, you may have to accept the situation and realize that money could be tight because of it. You may not be able to control your parent's desire to support you financially, but you can choose what kind of relationship you want to have with someone who abandons your support.

My stepbrother's real father buys him tons of things that I don't have. It's not fair that he lives with us but gets all that stuff from his dad.

Paul: Ken's has a huge stereo, tons of CDs, and the coolest guitar. He gets a gift or wads of cash whenever he visits his dad. I have to earn everything.

We invited Paul *and* Ken to meet to try to work out this issue. If Ken's dad has mega-money and wants to spend it on Ken, who's to argue? And if Paul *doesn't* have easy access to cash and stuff, nothing we say will change that. Money is a funny thing. It can really make enemies of people. Since Ken wasn't even aware of Paul's feelings, we asked Paul to begin by sharing them.

Paul acknowledged that his dad and stepmom (Ken's mom) provide all the necessities (like clothes, food, and an allowance). But he has to save for anything more (like a new stereo, concert tickets, or a snowboard). He explained that Ken gets the same as Paul from his mom and stepdad (Paul's dad), but that Ken's real dad buys him *everything* else he wants—he just has to ask. Paul admitted that even though he likes Ken, he is jealous that Ken doesn't have to earn anything.

After hearing Paul's side, Ken admitted that he did get lots of things from his father. But he explained that he feels his dad *owes* it to him. His father had abandoned him and his mother for many years. He eventually remarried a really nice woman, who must have told him to treat Ken better because Ken's dad suddenly started paying attention to him. At first Ken wanted to reject him the way he had been rejected. But then he realized that he should take whatever he could get from his father to make up for everything he had missed. So when his dad started offering him gifts, he gladly accepted, and still does.

When Paul realized that Ken's situation wasn't as straightforward as it had seemed, he didn't feel nearly as jealous. In fact, Ken even agreed to share all his stuff with Paul, which really helped, too. The fact that Paul and Ken were able to share their feelings went a long way to helping these stepsiblings get along better with each other.

What if it doesn't work . . . ?

Not all situations work out as easily as Ken and Paul's, although with open communication, understanding, and generosity, it's certainly possible. If your stepsibling gets tons of stuff from another parent and he or she doesn't want to share or even discuss it with you, you are going to have to search deep inside yourself to resolve the issue. The bottom line is that there is *always* going to be someone who has more money, more clothes, or a nicer car than you have. That's life. It's harder when it's someone you live with, but you still need to figure out a way not to be jealous or envious. These are destructive emotions that will eat away at you until you don't enjoy your own life. Instead be grateful for what you do have.

My dad says he can only pay for part of my college tuition because he's also paying for his stepkids' college. They're not his real children, so why do I have to lose out?

Ellen: My parents always told me I could go to any school I wanted, but now my dad's footing the bill for two more kids that aren't even his. I'm sure I won't be able to go to a good private college.

Time and again we see how money can change people's lives, and for Ellen it may limit her choice of colleges. For some kids, it may mean their parents won't be able to afford college at all. What most teens don't realize is that it's tough for their parents, too. It's not easy to find that the savings you planned to give to your kids must be spent differently. But as you know, life doesn't always go as planned. There are many different ways that divorce, death, and remarriage can have an impact on a family's financial situation.

Here are the main ones:

☞ Legal costs of a divorce.

☞ Medical costs for a dying spouse.

☞ Costs of maintaining two households after a divorce.

☞ Loss of one salary and the cost of childcare after one parent's death.

☞ Remarrying someone who needs help paying off big bills.

☞ Remarrying someone with kids who are not
   getting child support.

☞ Adopting stepkids whose other parent died or
   abandoned them.

It's not easy to realize your future might be
affected dramatically by a shake-up in your parents'
financial situation, and it's particularly difficult when
your loss is a stepsibling's gain. This is when you
need to recognize that life doesn't always go as
planned. Sometimes being angry prevents you from
seeing the big picture.

Take Ellen's situation, for example. She doesn't
understand why she has to suffer because her dad
chooses to send his stepkids to college. But if Ellen
stops to think, she'll realize that her stepsibs
wouldn't be able to go to college *at all* if it wasn't
for their mom marrying Ellen's dad. In other words,
Ellen may have to accept less than she would have,
but it's still more than her stepsiblings would
otherwise have had. Ellen could almost look at her

sacrifice as a good deed. If she is gracious, it will be appreciated, and she will feel good about helping someone else. If she is bitter, it could become a wedge between her and her father because he loves his wife and probably her children. Ellen's father feels bad that he can't give her everything she wants, but he also realizes that there's more to life than money. Relationships and family count for a lot, too. Besides, if Ellen can clear her mind of anger and resentment, it will be possible for her to get a lot more from college, no matter where she goes. If you're in the same situation as Ellen, these ideas may help you:

☞ Try to earn a scholarship to make college more affordable.

☞ Apply for financial aid and work-study programs.

☞ Strive for excellent grades in a less prestigious school so you rise to the top.

☞ Consider transferring colleges if things change financially.

☞ Get very good grades and then apply to top graduate schools after college.

There may not be one specific money issue—like choice of college—that affects you. You may feel you're being deprived of other things because of your stepsiblings' needs. For example, maybe there's less money for clothes, CDs, movies, or sports equipment. You probably won't be able to change the finances but it's still important to speak to your mom or dad about your feelings. Your parent will be able to explain why certain financial decisions have been made and how these decisions will affect you now and in the future. He or she may also help you seek alternate ways to meet your goals. For example, your parent could help you find a part-time job so you have more cash, and may even agree to drive you to and from work. The more you communicate, the better chance you have of getting your needs met.

What if it doesn't work . . . ?

Once in a while, a parent blatantly favors a stepchild financially in a way that substantially alters your lifestyle. There can be many reasons for this, including: feeling sorry for the child, wanting to win him or her over, or your parent wanting to prove his or her love to the new spouse. Under these circumstances, you should find out exactly what you can expect from your parent financially, and then accept what you are told. You will then have to figure out if there are other people (your other parent, grandparents, even aunts or uncles) who would be willing to help you through college or with other important goals requiring substantial money (e.g., school-related sports equipment, clothes, etc.). You may also need to get a part-time job, and you should plan to use at least part of that money to fund your future. This is a difficult concept for a teenager to have to think about, but the choices you make now can dramatically affect your future, and you will need to consider all your options carefully and realistically.

My dad used to buy me whatever I wanted. But his new wife told him he's spoiling me, so now he doesn't even want to pay for a school notebook. Why is she suddenly in charge of his money?

Glen: My stepmother is so greedy, she wants my dad to spend all his money on her. She told him I'm a spoiled brat, so he cut me off altogether. I wish she'd mind her own business!

Glen and his sister, Lydia, can't stand Merrill, their stepmother, and it has everything to do with money!

"Before Merrill came along, spending was never an issue, as long as we were reasonable," explained Lydia. "But now my dad won't spend a penny without her permission, and she never says yes to us."

"It seems like she does it just to spite our mom and us," continued Glen. "And my

dad doesn't see what's going on. It's
so infuriating!"

This reminded us of another family. In this family,
the stepmother, Danni, complained that her husband,
Lloyd, overindulged his kids constantly and they took
advantage, were rude, and generally treated him
with no respect. He worked all the time to make
enough money to give his kids everything they asked
for because if he didn't, they'd threaten to stop
visiting or speaking to him. When Danni married
Lloyd, she realized that his children were running
him ragged. He was scared to lose what little
contact he had with them, but he didn't realize that
giving them money was not really a relationship.

Danni helped Lloyd see that his children needed
him to be a good father, which included saying no
sometimes. The kids weren't happy about losing all
the stuff and money, nor were they thrilled that their
father was no longer eager to please them all the
time. They blamed Danni for "ruining things" for
them. They were sure she just wanted everything for

herself. It took a long time, as well as family therapy, for them to see that their dad needed to change his relationship with them whether Danni had encouraged it or not. We told this story to Glen and Lydia because we wondered if it was possible that their view of their stepmother might also be a bit harsh.

"Well," acknowledged Lydia, "my mom sometimes tells me to ask my dad to buy things for us—sneakers, skis, and my violin—even though it's in the agreement that she will get those things." Lydia began to cry. "Merrill says my dad gives my mom a lot of money but he still keeps paying and paying for everything. Sometimes I don't know who to believe." Glen and Lydia are definitely stuck in the middle. Their stepmother says that their mother takes advantage of their father. But their mother says that Merrill stands in the way of their dad giving them what he should.

This is a confusing situation, and if you feel you're similarly stuck, keep this in mind: You can't always assume your stepparent is out to get you.

Sometimes when a stepparent is new to a family, he or she sees things that should be changed. This is particularly true when the issues are about money because, as we have seen, having or not having money can bring out negative feelings in adults and teens. Parents sometimes give their children money and gifts as a way to deal with their own guilt about a divorce, or because they feel sorry that their child's other parent died. Of course this is not a healthy or satisfactory way to deal with such important feelings, and your stepparent, who is separate from these emotions, may realize this. So your stepparent may encourage your parent to change things in a way that you may not like (because it means you may get less money or gifts). But this doesn't mean the changes are bad for the family or for your long-term relationship with your mom or dad. It might be difficult to see this at first, but it's important for you to look at the situation as objectively as possible so you don't automatically alienate yourself from your stepparent.

On the other hand, it is not right for your

stepparent to bad-mouth your other parent, no matter what the reason. If you hear this happening, you should discuss it with the parent to whom your step is married. The adults need to work out these money issues privately, without burdening you.

What if it doesn't work . . . ?

If you *really* believe your stepparent is greedy, you will need to do your best to get your parent to see things for what they are. To do this you will need "hard evidence" that you are being treated unfairly. When talking to your parent, cite specific examples of how things have changed since the remarriage. Remind your parent that in the past they did not deny you money when your requests were reasonable, and that you feel this is no longer the case. It would definitely be better to have this conversation privately with your mom or dad so that you have an uninterrupted chance to make your point.

Chapter Eight
Really Sticky Situations

There are times when living in a stepfamily can be particularly difficult. You may have to be prepared to handle situations that make you feel really weird, uncomfortable, or even scared. It helps to know that you're not the only one who's had experiences like these.

My father and his girlfriend live together. How do I tell them I wish they would get married?

Roy: I'm really embarrassed that my dad and his live-in girlfriend aren't married. Sometimes I just lie and tell people they are.

It is understandable that Roy is uncomfortable with this setup, but there are many different reasons people decide not to marry right away (or sometimes at all). We spoke to some adults who are living with someone and found out the reasons they're not married:

✖ **We're not sure we're ready for the commitment, but we want to try it out.**

✖ **It's less expensive to live together.**

✖ **We want to be together, but I don't want to subject my kids to another divorce if it doesn't work out.**

✖ **I'm not officially divorced so I can't get married yet. The divorce could take years, and we don't want to wait to live together.**

✖ **We're planning the wedding, so it's not so bad.**

✖ My first wife died, and I'm afraid it could happen again, but I don't want to live alone.

As you can see, there are many different reasons adults choose to live together without getting married. If you talk to your parent about why he or she is living with someone, perhaps understanding the reasons will make it easier for you to accept this choice. Of course, there are also many reasons kids don't like the situation, so we asked some teens to tell us why they're unhappy about it. Here are their reasons.

✖ It's embarrassing to tell my friends.

✖ It makes me worry they won't stay together.

✖ Is she my stepmother or not?

✖ What if my mom gets pregnant and they're not married?

✖ They're always telling me "no sex before you're married," so how come it's okay for them?

These are all *very* legitimate concerns, so we'll try to tackle them one at a time:

It's embarrassing. You are not living with someone, so there's nothing for you to be embarrassed about. In other words, separate yourself from your parents. If you don't like it, tell your friends that you don't agree with your parent's choice but there's nothing you can do about it. It's probably not a great idea to pretend they are married (even though it seems easier) because you will always worry that the truth will come out, and then you really *will* have something to be embarrassed about!

They won't stay together. This is a common worry when your parent lives with someone without getting married. If you've already been through a divorce, it's especially worrying because you know it could happen again. You definitely need to talk to your parent about your fears. Maybe they'll explain that they intend to marry, which will help you relax a bit. Even if they tell you there is a chance it won't work out, at least you can prepare yourself.

Is she my stepmother? It can be confusing if you don't know what to think of your parent's live-in girlfriend or boyfriend. After a parent's death, many kids would love to have a stepparent, and it can be frustrating if your parent doesn't get married. In a situation like this, it would be great to talk to the girlfriend or boyfriend directly and discuss some different ways the two of you could think of your relationship. You will probably feel relieved afterward, although you still won't have an "official" stepparent.

What if my mom gets pregnant? This is a tough one, but the bottom line here is that it's not really something you can control. You have to hope that your mom or dad is responsible enough to have thought out all the consequences of getting pregnant. Some adults don't think it's a big deal to have a baby without being married. If this is the case in your family, you'll have to accept it. If you don't agree, you won't make the same choices when you're an adult.

What about "no sex before marriage"? This is a tough one also because you're right; it's definitely a double standard in some ways. One way of looking at it is that your parent has already had sex and even children. Your parent's decision to remain a sexually active adult is not as monumental as it would be for you to have sex as a teenager for the first time. If it seems like a religious double standard, you will have to accept your parent's choice to have sex outside of marriage (and possibly even before he or she is officially divorced). But if you feel strongly about waiting until you're married, there's no reason to follow in your parent's footsteps. It's important not to make an impulsive decision to have sex just to "get back at" you mom or dad. And if you are sexually active, you might think about whether you did it just "to spite" them or if it is something you really want for yourself.

Also, the truth is, your parent's private life is really not up for discussion. Just as you don't discuss all the choices you make, you owe them the same privacy when it comes to their sex life. It's a tough subject, but if it really bothers you, try to talk to your parent about their choice to have sex outside of marriage. It may help you to hear their side, and hearing your side would give them something to think about.

What if it doesn't work . . . ?

Perhaps you live in a very small town or a very religious community. Or perhaps you have been the victim of teasing or bullying in school and this would make things much worse for you. In rare circumstances like these, you may be left with no choice but to pretend your parent is married. Do so very carefully and be sure you don't get caught in the lie. If you do, you may be very embarrassed and possibly get into trouble. However, if you truly believe you will be victimized for sharing the truth, pretending may be your only option. If living with your other parent is an option, you may also want to consider it, but only after you talk with your parents.

I have a serious crush on my stepsister. Is there something wrong with me?

> ***Tony:*** My stepsister is really hot and I think about her all the time. But it's really freaky that I'm feeling this way, I mean we're *related*.

Attraction to a stepsister or stepbrother is definitely difficult to handle. We discussed it in a stepteen group, and you'd be surprised how many kids admitted to having felt just like Tony.

> ***Mac:*** My stepsister and I actually kissed once, but then we decided it would only lead to trouble so we made a pact to end it. We talked about it the other day, and we're both glad we made that agreement.

> ***Cara:*** I think my stepbrother is so great, and I always imagine what it would be like if we were together, but he's not at all interested in me in "that" way. So it's my big secret.

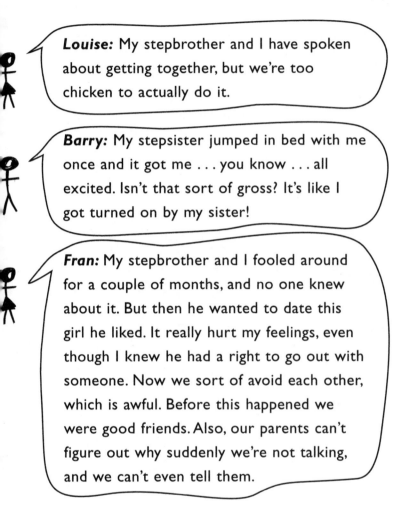

Louise: My stepbrother and I have spoken about getting together, but we're too chicken to actually do it.

Barry: My stepsister jumped in bed with me once and it got me . . . you know . . . all excited. Isn't that sort of gross? It's like I got turned on by my sister!

Fran: My stepbrother and I fooled around for a couple of months, and no one knew about it. But then he wanted to date this girl he liked. It really hurt my feelings, even though I knew he had a right to go out with someone. Now we sort of avoid each other, which is awful. Before this happened we were good friends. Also, our parents can't figure out why suddenly we're not talking, and we can't even tell them.

As you can see, some teens fantasize about it, some talk about it, some test it out, and some actually give in to their feelings for each other. So clearly you're not alone if you have sexual feelings for a stepsibling. But this type of attraction usually provokes all sorts of conflicting feelings. Most teens we asked said they felt excited, guilty, confused, embarrassed, and freakish. So let's try to address some of these feelings by dispelling some myths.

<u>**Myth:**</u> There's something wrong with me if I have sexual feelings for a stepsibling because we're related.

Fact: You're only related by chance, not by blood or family. If your parents hadn't gotten together, your step would be just another kid of the opposite sex who you thought was cute. Becoming "siblings" won't necessarily make your attraction or physical excitement go away, and it doesn't mean there's anything wrong with you, either.

Myth: I can't tell anyone that I'm attracted to my stepsibling.

Fact: It may not be wise to tell *everyone* you have sexual feelings for a stepsib, but it is certainly okay (and even a good idea) to tell one adult you can trust. It can be a relief not to have to keep the secret and maybe a parent, counselor, or other trusted adult can help you understand your feelings. It's probably not a great idea to talk to friends about it, though. They may be just as confused as you are, and their advice may not be sound.

Myth: True love can be found anywhere, so it's okay for us to get involved.

Fact: There is a lot more to a meaningful, long-term relationship than physical attraction or even really, really liking someone. Being stepsiblings means that you have to live in the same house and share the same parents for a long time. If your relationship doesn't work out (most teens go out with someone for a few months and then break up), you will be stuck with having to live with the person you broke up with. Not a great situation!

As you can see, it is not always easy to control your sexual feelings for a stepsibling but at the same time, it's probably not the best idea to act on them. So how do you go about avoiding trouble?

Here are a few tips:

☞ If you have feelings for a stepsibling, acknowledge it to yourself and don't act on them impulsively.

☞ If your feelings are reciprocated, discuss with your stepsib how it might feel to get involved while living in the same house (remember what Mac and Fran said).

☞ Resist kissing, touching, or other behavior that may turn you both on. It's much harder to stop once you've started, and there's a good chance you'll regret it afterward.

☞ If you're already involved, you should seriously consider stopping—even if you don't want to. In all likelihood, you will find yourselves at odds before long.

☞ Try the test of time. If your romantic feelings for each other are real, they won't go away. Once you hit adulthood and are no longer in the same house as "siblings," you can reassess whether you want to be together. Remember, there's nothing "wrong" with becoming involved, but it will definitely make your stepfamily situation much more complicated. The two of you can always try romance later on.

What if it doesn't work . . . ?

If you are already heavily sexually involved with a stepsibling, the two of you need to speak to an adult. Learn how to avoid being hurt by each other and how to make things less stressful at home. You don't necessarily have to speak to your parents if you think they couldn't handle it, but you should definitely get together with a counselor, therapist, or other trusted adult. Furthermore, if your sexual involvement includes intercourse or other very intimate sexual acts, you must speak to a doctor about birth control and contraception against sexually transmitted diseases such as HIV and herpes. Becoming sexually involved, particularly with someone in your own home, can be complicated to say the least, so it's very important for both of you to get some guidance.

My stepfather walks around the house in his underwear or even with no clothes on, and I'm mortified!

> **Tanya:** I'm afraid to come out of my room because if I run into my stepfather in his underwear, it totally grosses me out. Why does he have to do that?

Sometimes parents and stepparents walk around in underwear, or nude, in front of opposite sex children or stepchildren. Some kids aren't bothered by it (especially if it's their parent or a stepparent they've known since they were tiny). Others are freaked out if a parent or a stepparent does this. Some are bothered only if it's a stepparent. We don't know for sure why your stepparent walks around in underwear (or totally naked!) but let's assume for now that it's because he or she is comfortable this way and doesn't realize it really bothers you. Your first step should be to tell your parent and your stepparent how uncomfortable it makes you. Your stepparent is probably unaware how you feel. Perhaps you're the first teenager they've lived with. If it helps, you can even explain that it's not a "stepparent" issue, but rather a general feeling that you'd rather not see an opposite sex body so casually exposed. Most stepparents will respond appropriately to this by covering themselves up while in your presence and saving their "state of undress" for behind closed doors.

Unfortunately, there are some stepparents (and parents) who don't use good sense when it comes to exposing their bodies to you in a way that clearly makes you uncomfortable. If your stepparent becomes angry or insulted that you have a problem with his or her nudity, you can probably assume you have this type of stepparent. In a situation like this, you need to recognize that your stepparent is violating boundaries of comfortable and appropriate behavior. You have a right to be upset by this. You don't have the power to enforce a change, but your parent does. *So, you must make it very clear to your parent that you are extremely uncomfortable in the house under these circumstances.* Ask your parent to do his or her best to convince your stepparent to behave more modestly. Try to have the conversation seriously, without crying or losing your temper. You will have a much greater impact on your parent if your parent realizes that you are approaching this in a mature, controlled manner.

What if it doesn't work . . . ?

☞ If it isn't the home you live in, you can refuse to visit unless things change.

☞ If it is the home you live in, you should avoid the situation as much as possible. For example, if your stepparent usually walks around in his or her underwear (or naked) at night, stay in your room or go to a friend's house. If it is feasible, you might consider moving in with your other parent.

☞ Talk to a guidance counselor, school psychologist, or social worker.

☞ Recognize that this behavior is inappropriate and don't allow your parent or stepparent to blame you for being uncomfortable.

When my stepfather puts his arm around me, I feel really uncomfortable. My mom says I'm overreacting because he's like a father. To me, he seems more like a guy than a father.

Chloe: I feel like running every time my stepfather comes near me. He touches me all the time and it totally grosses me out. I wish he'd just stay away.

There are a number of issues in Chloe's situation that need to be addressed.

1. Why does Chloe feel uncomfortable?

2. Should her mother take her more seriously?

3. Why does her stepfather touch her like that?

4. Can this happen to boys?

5. What if he does more than just put his arm around her?

We will address these issues one at a time because we want to be sure that you understand all about good and bad touching. We also want you to know how to handle touches that you may not understand or like.

1. Chloe probably feels uncomfortable because her stepfather is not actually her parent. Having his arm around her probably feels too intimate for the type of relationship they have. Her feelings are completely valid. In fact—and this is important—

everybody is entitled to ask someone to stop any type of touching that doesn't feel good or right. Whether it is a parent, stepparent, friend, boyfriend, girlfriend, sibling, stepsibling, cousin, grandparent, aunt, uncle, acquaintance, or stranger (or anyone else we may have left out!)—you do not have to let any of these people touch you in a way that doesn't feel good.

2. Chloe's mother should certainly take her daughter's concerns seriously. In all likelihood, she doesn't want Chloe to feel uneasy because she knows that Chloe's stepdad is just trying to be friendly and "dad-like." However, this doesn't mean that Chloe has to accept the closeness if it feels uncomfortable. If your parent doesn't seem to be hearing what you are saying, you need to make your point more clearly. Tell your mom or dad that your stepmother or stepfather is getting too close physically and that you don't like it. Say that you're not ready for such an intimate relationship, and that it's not going to make you feel closer to your step. Ask your mom or dad to speak to your stepparent about your feelings.

3. Chloe's stepdad is probably trying to build a close, parenting relationship with her. Perhaps he thinks it will make them closer if he puts his arm around her sometimes. If this seems to be happening in your relationship with a stepparent, you might be able to talk to him or her about it. Explain that you want to have a close relationship, but that you're not ready for so much touchy-feely stuff.

4. Yes, this can certainly happen to boys. Boys can be just as uncomfortable as girls if their stepmother or stepfather touches them too much or in a way that doesn't feel good. They should be just as open and honest with their stepparent and parent about not liking it.

5. In rare circumstances, stepparents touch their stepchildren for reasons that are not about parenting. If you feel that your stepparent is touching you because it is sexually exciting for him or her, or if it feels like the touching seems to be getting increasingly intimate or more frequent, YOU NEED TO TALK TO SOMEONE ABOUT IT IMMEDIATELY.

If you can, talk to your parent, although it's possible that your parent won't believe you. You may need to tell a school counselor, teacher, or other trusted adult. This is not something you should keep secret. If you are mistaken, the adults will work it out. But if your gut feeling is correct and your stepparent is making sexual advances, you can stop it before something bad happens to you. Bad things include touching or rubbing you anywhere that feels too intimate, like your back, stomach, legs, breasts, or inside your underwear. If something bad does happen, and you don't have an adult to talk to—or if no one believes you—call the police and tell them what happened. You can also call Child Protective Services or Child Welfare (it may have a slightly different name where you live). You can get the number from the operator or look it up in the big white pages phone book. It's usually in the front part of the phone book, and it's a toll-free number.

What if it doesn't work . . . ?

If your stepparent won't stop putting an arm

around you or touching you in ways that don't feel right, you might need to avoid being around your stepparent as much as possible. Spend time with friends, with your other parent (if you can), or simply in other parts of your home. Don't sit near your stepparent and try not to get close enough for him or her to put an arm around you. You might seem cold, but he or she needs to learn to respect your request for him or her to back off.

My mom got divorced and now she's gay!

> **Chelsey:** My parents divorced, and now my mom is living with another woman. I'm staying with my dad because I just can't deal with it!

As hard as it is to adjust to a stepfamily, it's even harder to adjust to a parent becoming involved with someone of the same sex.

1. My dad suddenly seems like a whole new person and I'm not sure what to make of it.

Well, actually your mom or dad is not really a new person, he or she is just expressing something that until now has been kept a secret. Your parent is probably relieved to finally be letting it show. Divorce doesn't make someone gay. However, it does give parents an opportunity to explore part of their personality that was there all along. It is possible that the divorce happened *because* your parent could no longer stay in a heterosexual relationship. It's also possible that your parent is trying out a homosexual relationship to see how it feels, and that he or she may end up in another heterosexual relationship eventually. (Although, if your parent has been with the same person for a long time, it is probably not just experimentation.)

2. How can I have the same relationship with my mom now?

Your parents' sexual choices don't have anything to do with the way they relate to you. Once you get used to things, there is no reason to expect that your relationship with your mom or dad should change at all. Your mom or dad is still the same person and the same parent.

3. It grosses me out to see my dad holding hands with another man.

This is understandable. It will take time to get used to it. You can ask your mom or dad not to do that sort of thing until you have had some time to adjust to the relationship. Your parent will probably be very understanding if you are not hostile or rude in your request.

4. I don't want to live with them.

If you have somewhere else to live, it may be an option worth considering. It may be easier to get used to the idea that your parent is gay if you can do it gradually rather than being confronted by it on a daily basis.

5. Does it mean that I'm gay?

No, your parent's sexual orientation has nothing to do with you. However, many people have homosexual feelings at some point in their life. Sometimes it is just a passing phase. But if you really do think you're gay, you have a parent who will be understanding and willing to talk to you about it. Being gay is not wrong, it's just another way of living that is no more right or wrong than any other way.

6. Does this mean that my mom never wanted to have me in the first place?

Being gay has nothing to do with wanting to have children. In fact, many gay couples do have or adopt children because they want them just as much as heterosexual couples. Your relationship with your mom or dad is just as stable and secure as it was before you found out he or she was gay.

7. I'll never be able to accept it.

Never is a very long time. There are many things that children and parents do that are difficult to deal with. But when we love each other, we figure out a way to overcome our confused or angry feelings. Your mom or dad has made a choice to live a different kind of life because it makes him or her much happier. Of course, it will be a very difficult adjustment for you and the rest of the family. But it will have a negative impact on you only if you let it. In a few years you will be an adult and living your own life. Your mom or dad can't make all their decisions based on what makes *you* happy. This is something you can get used to if you give yourself a chance.

What if it doesn't work . . . ?

If the whole thing seems completely overwhelming to you, and you can't seem to get over how much it has disrupted your life, tell your mom or dad that you would like to speak to a therapist. It is very important that you learn to cope with your new reality, and a therapist (psychologist, social worker, counselor) can be a real lifesaver in this type of situation. This is not a time to be embarrassed to ask for help. It can be a really stressful life change, and you should get all the help you can.

A Final Thought

Now that you've finished reading the book, you realize there are many different solutions to the problems you might find in your stepfamily. You can also see that you're not the only teenager whose stepfamily situation is sometimes stressful and confusing. Although things won't always go the way you want, you don't have to sit around feeling sorry for yourself. Like all the teens in this book, you **can** make the best of your situation. The best might not be perfect, but it will almost always be better. And here's another important consideration: If you can use what you've learned in this book to make your stepfamily a more comfortable place to live, you will see that you can be in control of your life.

About the Authors

Joel Block, Ph.D. is a clinical psychologist practicing couple, family and individual psychotherapy on Long Island, New York. A diplomate of the American Board of Professional Psychology, Dr. Block is a supervisor on the staff of Long Island Jewish Medical Center and an Assistant Clinical Professor at the Einstein College of Medicine. He is the author of numerous magazine articles and nine books including: *Broken Promises, Mended Hearts, Friendship, Lasting Love*, and *To Marry Again*. Dr. Block lives and practices in Huntington, New York.

Dr. Susan S. Bartell is a licensed psychologist who works extensively with teenagers, as well as with parents and children who are coping with divorce and remarriage. Dr. Bartell has a private practice in Port Washington, New York.

She also maintains a website, **www.havinganotherbaby.com** which helps families, including stepfamilies, prepare for a new baby and manage sibling rivalry.